HEAVEN
COMING
DOWN

HEAVEN COMING DOWN

Because Heaven Came Down

SANDRA MACKEY

XULON PRESS

Unless otherwise indicated, Scripture quotations and references are taken from the Holy Bible, New International Version®, NIV® Copyright © 1973, 1978, 1984, 2011 by Biblica, Inc. ® Used by permission. All rights reserved worldwide.

Other books by Sandra Mackey:
Better Than Gold and Silver
Poems of Love and Faith
The Spirit of Truth
When Righteousness and Peace Kiss

Available from:
sandramackey11@gmail.com
https://sandramackey.com
https://www.facebook.com/sandra.mackey1

Printed in the United States of America.

ISBN: 978-1-7327240-3-7 – (soft cover)
ISBN: 978-1-7327240-4-4 – (digital)

Xulon Press
2301 Lucien Way #415
Maitland, FL 32751
407.339.4217
www.xulonpress.com

Sandra is a gifted writer, a wonderful friend, and my treasured sister in Christ. Her spiritual passion and courageous inquiry oozes out of these pages. From creation to new creation, Sandra draws us into the giant vision of God for his beloved world. The reader will be informed and inspired, but also challenged and transformed. You cannot make it through this book without wrestling with the Biblical truth and important questions Sandra presents. As I read, I found myself asking, *So, what is God's future for the world?* and, *What does God expect of me in light of our present redemption and future restoration?* As you read, take notes, reflect, and pray. Seek the Lord with all your heart and lean not on your own understanding, and you will be richly blessed.

Love First,

Don McLaughlin

Author – Love First: *Ending Hate Before It's Too Late*

Senior Minister, North Atlanta Church of Christ

Atlanta, Georgia

Sandra Mackey is a very dear sister in Christ. She loves the Word, she loves the Lord and she loves His people. Sandra loves to encourage people in their walk with Jesus and to remind us that this life is temporary and that we will always be with the Lord. Read this book with an open heart. You'll be glad you did.

Dr. Mark Richardson

Pastoral Counselor; Life Coach

Author – *Return to Innocence* and *52 Days on the Wall*

Atlanta, Georgia

DEDICATION

²⁰ Now to him who is able to do immeasurably more than all we ask or imagine, according to his power that is at work within us, ²¹ to him be glory in the church and in Christ Jesus throughout all generations, for ever and ever! Amen. (Ephesians 3:20).

CONTENTS

FOREWORD

AS MY RESEARCH FOR THIS BOOK BEGAN IN 2018, IT CAME as an unimaginable surprise that there are over 6,054 books already written about heaven! That does not include the Bible! It does not include the hundreds of YouTube videos of people who have their own ideas of what heaven will be like. It also does not include the many "near-death-experiences" with visions of heaven that are recorded. So, what in heaven's name could I possibly have to say that would be different or more enlightening than those other 6,054 books?

I read quite a few of those books and found quite a few different theories. Many did not agree with the others. Nevertheless, I had been contemplating this writing for several months, and I decided that if the Holy Spirit was leading me, it would be done. But please allow me to advise you, dear reader, that my standard for life and eternity resides within the pages of only one book, the Holy Bible, because,

"16 All Scripture is God-breathed and is useful for teaching, rebuking, correcting and training in righteousness..." (2 Timothy 3:16).

Therefore, for the most part, my research has not been from the media or books of prophecy written by novelists, but my research has primarily been from the Bible and Bible dictionaries, concordances, and commentaries from reliable sources that I trust to be as accurate as possible. Writing from faith without knowledge is always a challenge but writing from faith that is confident in the scriptures is easier. (Hebrews 11:1). And let's face it... none of us will have all the answers until we see the face of Jesus.

To be totally honest, I have not always been excited about the prospect of heaven… mainly because I was afraid that I could never be good enough to end up there. But heaven was a daily topic of conversation in my family growing up, and daily prayers about wanting to go there, so it was a frequent reminder that everyone dies, then what?

To illustrate, my earliest memories are when I was three years old. That's totally irrelevant, but I know it because I had my tonsils and adenoids removed when I was three, and I vividly remember being in the hospital bed with my mother and father standing beside me.

I also remember my bedtime prayer when I was three:

"Now I lay me down to sleep, I pray the Lord my soul to keep; if I should die before I wake, I pray the Lord my soul to take."

I'm not sure how much older I was when I began asking questions about my prayers. Looking back, it seems that I usually asked my dad questions, because my mother always sent me to him for answers anyway, because he was very smart, she said.

"Daddy, where is God taking my soul? What's a soul anyway?"

I remember that he put his hands on either side of my face and looked me in the eyes and said, "Sandy, God gave you a body to live in while you are alive on this earth, (patting my head) but your soul is the part of you that belongs to him. We can't see it, but we know it's there. And one day when you are very old and don't need your body any more, then he will take your soul to where he lives -- to heaven -- because he loves you and wants you to live with him forever and ever. And your mama and I will be there too. It will be the most beautiful place we have ever seen!" And I knew it was true, because my daddy said so.

Since then, I've had time to think about the beauty of heaven, but somewhere along my journey, I learned about the fires of hell, and I spent more than too many years worried about going to hell. You see, I had not yet learned about God's love, grace and mercy through the sacrifice of his son, Jesus.

Today, realizing that almost four-score years have passed in my life-time, and that I am beginning to see that time of being "very old," I would like to invite you to join me on this incredible spiritual journey that in a few years will be over for me on earth, but just beginning for me in heaven for eternity.

This is what we will study together:

1. THE CREATION OF GOD - God's creation, the beginning of the heavens and the earth.
2. THE ATTRIBUTES OF GOD - The omni-attributes of God; his omnipotence, omniscience and omni-presence: this all-powerful, all-knowing, and always everywhere three-in-one Father, Son, and Holy Spirit.
3. THE WORD OF GOD - The Bible as God's word as the source of our understanding and hope.
4. THE KINGDOM OF GOD – God's reign on earth and in heaven.
5. THE SON OF GOD - The glory of Jesus Christ coming down from heaven to be a sacrifice for our sins.
6. THE PLAN OF GOD - What the Bible says about Christian eschatology, the study of "end times."
7. THE NEW CREATION OF GOD - John's Revelation of his vision of heaven. We will be reading and learning about the *new heavens and the new earth*. (Revelation 21). You may be familiar with many of these verses, but I urge you to step into a new vision of things-to-come and investigate with pure eyes everything you have learned in the past and thought you knew about heaven.
8. THE PROMISE OF GOD - Our faith and hope in God's promise that he wants to be with his children.
9. What major religions think about heaven.
10. Unusual near-death experiences.

Try to acknowledge with caution what you have read in books, seen in movies, art, or imagination as being what they are -- someone's attempt, even my own, to bring the unimaginable to reality. Doing so does not make any of us wrong about what we believe about heaven today; but it may, hopefully, expand our conscious thoughts about heaven.

We will be reading copious verses of scripture. Those will be the most important parts of this book. Be sure to not skip over them because you feel as though you already know what those verses say. Read them afresh with your eyes and your heart. (The lines of scripture that are typed in bold are my emphases).

Within the next few pages, I hope that I will be able to convey my excitement about the nearness of heaven and the anticipation of crossing over into eternity when I will awaken to see the face of Jesus as I bow before the throne of God. Perhaps it will also allow you to envision **Heaven Coming Down,** because Heaven came down in the form of the son of God, Jesus, the Christ.

Bless us now, dear Lord God and Father, as we study together. Jesus, thank you for your sacrificial love. Now, please guide our every word and thought with your Holy Spirit. Amen.

—Sandra Mackey

PREFACE

Word Studies

THESE ARE NOT MY DEFINITIONS. THEY COME FROM Merriam-Webster's online dictionary[1] and the Holy Bible.[2] I have merely grouped them according to topic. It is my opinion that a good understanding of the words we use will greatly assist in our study.

Bible
1. The sacred scriptures comprising the Old Testament and the New Testament
2. The sacred accounts of other religions (such as Judaism)
3. As in 2 Timothy 3:14-17

Firmament:
1. The vault or arch of the sky: heavens
2. The gaseous envelope of a celestial body (such as a planet)
3. The whole mass of air surrounding the earth

Heaven(s):
1. The expanse of space that seems to be over the earth like a dome: Firmament—usually used in plural
2. As in Genesis 1:1
3. Often capitalized: the dwelling place of the Deity and the blessed dead, as in Acts 1:9-11
4. A spiritual state of everlasting communion with God

Earth

1.   The fragmental material composing part of the surface of the globe especially: cultivable soil, as in Genesis 1:1
2.   The sphere of mortal life as distinguished from spheres of spirit life
3.   Areas of land as distinguished from sea and air
4.   The solid footing formed of soil: ground

Kingdom

1.   A politically organized community or major territorial unit having a monarchical form of government headed by a king or queen
2.   Often capitalized
3.   The eternal kingship of God
4.   The realm in which God's will is fulfilled

Prophet

1.   A forthteller; a speaker in present day telling of something yet to come
2.   One who utters divinely inspired revelations: such as writer of one of the prophetic books of the Bible
3.   One regarded by a group of followers as the final authoritative revealer of God's will,
4.   One gifted with more than ordinary spiritual and moral insight
5.   An effective or leading spokesman for a cause, doctrine, or group; as a teacher

Prophecy

1.   Forthtelling; speaking in present day of something yet to come
2.   An inspired utterance of a prophet
3.   The function or vocation of a prophet, specifically, the inspired declaration of divine will and purpose
4.   As the prophecy of the coming of Jesus – Isaiah 53

Revelation

1. An act of revealing or communicating divine truth
2. Something that is revealed by God to humans
3. An act of revealing to view or making known
4. Something that is revealed especially: an enlightening or astonishing disclosure
5. A pleasant often enlightening surprise
6. Capitalized: an apocalyptic writing addressed to early Christians of Asia Minor and included as a book in the New Testament

Jerusalem

1. City in southwestern Asia northwest of the Dead Sea
2. As in 1 Chronicles 23:25; Isaiah 2:3; Micah 4:2
3. Jerusalem is a holy city for Jews, Christians, and Muslims (Islam)

Zion

1. Or Mount Zion, or Sion; or Mount Sion hill in eastern Jerusalem, Israel, from where the word of the Lord was spoken. Isaiah 2:3

Church

1. A building for public and especially Christian worship
2. The clergy or officialdom of a religious body
3. A body or organization of religious believers; as in Matthew 16:18; Ephesians 4:15; Colossians 1:18
4. The whole body of Christians, as in Galatians 1:1
5. Prophecy of the Lord's church – Isaiah 2:2, 3
6. Bride of the Lamb – Hosea 2:16, 19, 20; 2 Corinthians 11:2; Revelation 21:2, 9

The New Jerusalem

1. The final abode of souls redeemed by Christ; Old Testament and New Testament
2. An ideal earthly community
3. As in Revelation 3:12; 19:7-9; 21:2, 9-10

1

GOD CREATED THE HEAVENS AND THE EARTH

Genesis, Chapters 1 – 3

¹In the beginning God created the heavens and the earth. ²Now the earth was formless and empty, darkness was over the surface of the deep, and the Spirit of God was hovering over the waters. (Genesis 1:1-2).

ON THE FIRST DAY, GOD MADE DAY AND NIGHT, LIGHT and darkness.

On the second day, God separated the water in the sky above from the waters below it.

On the third day, God separated the waters below the sky from the dry ground, calling them land and sea. The land produced vegetation, plants, and trees bearing fruit. And God saw that **it was good**.

On the fourth day, God made two great lights of the sky to give light on the earth, to govern the day and the night, and to separate light from darkness. And God saw that **it was good.**

On the fifth day, God created the great creatures of the sea and every living creature that moves about in the water, and birds in the sky. And God saw that **it was good**.

On the sixth day, God created livestock, wild animals, and all the creatures that move along the ground.

²⁶ Then God said, "Let us make mankind in our image, in our likeness, so that they may rule over the fish in the sea and the birds in the sky, over the livestock and all the wild animals, and over all the creatures that move along the ground."

God created mankind in his own image, male and female. He gave them rule over every living creature and gave all green plants, beasts, birds, and fish for food. And God saw all that he had made, and **it was very good.**

On the seventh day, God blessed the day and made it holy because on it he rested from all the work of creating that he had done.

How Many Heavens?

Genesis 1:1 says that God created "the heavens," plural. So how many heavens did God create? As a kindergarten astronomer, this is my understanding of the heavens about which we can read in the Bible:

The **first heaven** is the atmosphere around the earth. For example, in describing the rain that brought on the flood of Noah's time, we read, *¹¹ In the six hundredth year of Noah's life, on the seventeenth day of the second month—on that day all the springs of the great deep burst forth, and the **floodgates of the heavens were opened.** ¹² And rain fell on the earth** forty days and forty nights.* Genesis 7:11-12). God's throne is not in the first heaven.

The **second heaven** is commonly referred to as "outer space." Exodus 32:13 talks about "the stars in the sky." Stars are not in the skies from which the rain falls, but in the space beyond our atmosphere. Nehemiah 9:6 also refers to space as heaven: *⁶ You alone are the LORD. You made the heavens, even **the highest heavens, and all their starry host,** the earth and all that is on it, the seas and all that is in them. You give life to everything, and the multitudes of heaven worship you.* God's throne is not in the second heaven.

Paul, speaking of himself in a very modest third-person, said that a man he knew had gone to **the third heaven**, which he called **paradise,** and that he had seen and heard inexpressible things that could not be told. (2 Corinthians 12:1-4). It is apparent that the third heaven is described as paradise, the same place where Jesus told the thief on the cross that he would see him. Revelation 4:9-11 describes this third heaven as the location of the throne of God.

⁹ Whenever the living creatures give glory, honor and thanks to him who sits on the throne and who lives for ever and ever, ¹⁰ the twenty-four elders fall down before him who sits on the throne and worship him who lives for ever and ever. They lay their crowns before the throne and say:

¹¹ "You are worthy, our Lord and God,
*   to receive glory and honor and power,*
for you created all things,
*   and by your will they were created*
*   and have their being."*

Eden Was Very Good but Not Perfect

Thinking about heaven, we may hear someone say that heaven will be perfect if it is like things were in the beginning of creation; in the Garden of Eden before Eve and Adam sinned. Upon closer observation, we will see that the Garden of Eden was not perfect. Satan had been cast out of heaven sometime before (Luke 10:18) and was in Eden seeking to beguile and deceive these new humans, which he did.

We have seen thousands of years since then; full of wars, holy wars, and rumors of wars; of disasters, murders, sin and consequences of sin throughout history. However, God did not make his creation to be permanently like this. He had much more in store for his creation. Even **before the creation** he had purposed more for us through Jesus.

So maybe think of it like this: We are living in the first heavens and first earth, with the new heavens and new earth yet to come. THEN we will have perfection!!

*³ Praise be to the God and Father of our Lord Jesus Christ, who has blessed us in the heavenly realms with every spiritual blessing in Christ. ⁴ For he chose us in him **before the creation of the world** to be holy and blameless in his sight. In love ⁵ he predestined us for adoption to son-ship through Jesus Christ, in accordance with his pleasure and will.* (Ephesians 1:3-6).

Adam and Eve and Two Trees in the Garden of Eden

The Bible tells us that God created the heavens and the earth and everything in it. He created the first man, Adam, from dust of the ground, and from Adam's rib he created the first woman, Eve. (Genesis 2:7, 21). God put them in the Garden of Eden to care and nurture the land. He told Adam and Eve that they could eat any fruit from the trees except for the tree of the knowledge of good and evil. God warned them that if they ate from that tree they would die.

⁸ Now the LORD God had planted a garden in the east, in Eden; and there he put the man he had formed.

⁹ The LORD God made all kinds of trees grow out of the ground—trees that were pleasing to the eye and good for food. In the middle of the garden were the tree of life and the tree of the knowledge of good and evil --

¹⁵ The LORD God took the man and put him in the Garden of Eden to work it and take care of it. ¹⁶ And the LORD God commanded the man, "You are free to eat from any tree in the garden; ¹⁷ but you must not eat from the tree of the knowledge of good and evil, for when you eat from it you will certainly die." (Genesis 2:8-9, 15-17).

More About Satan

One day Satan came disguised as a serpent and spoke to Eve, convincing her to eat the fruit from the tree of the knowledge of good and evil. Eve told the serpent that God said they should not eat it, and that they would die if they did, but Satan tempted Eve to eat, saying that she would become like God if she did. Eve believed the lie and took a bite of the fruit. She then gave some to Adam for him to eat. Adam and Eve, now knowing that they had sinned, immediately felt ashamed and tried to hide from God.

These acts gave them additional knowledge, but they also gave them the ability to conjure negative and destructive concepts such as shame and evil. We see that there were consequences of their sin. God had told them they would die if they ate of the tree of the knowledge of good and evil. He cursed the serpent to go on his belly and suffer the enmity of both man and woman. He cursed the ground so the man would have a lifetime of hard labor. And, as a consequence of her sin, the woman would have pain in childbirth and be submissive to her husband.

God clothed the nakedness of the man and woman, who had become god-like in knowing good and evil, then he banished them from the garden lest they eat the fruit of a second tree, the tree of life, and live forever.

22 And the LORD God said, "The man has now become like one of us, knowing good and evil. He must not be allowed to reach out his hand and take also from the tree of life and eat and live forever."23 So the LORD God banished him from the Garden of Eden to work the ground from which he had been taken. 24 After he drove the man out, he placed on the east side of the Garden of Eden cherubim and a flaming sword flashing back and forth to guard the way to the tree of life. (Genesis 3:22-24).

As a result of their sin, Adam and Eve were separated from God, and they lost their access to the tree of life. They had messed up their lives and the lives of all humanity who have followed since then.

When Satan had successfully tempted Adam and Eve, he not only brought the human family into the life and death struggle that we experience today, but now as a result of mankind's fall, Satan had obtained authority over the whole earth. Satan began claiming the earth as the place where he rules. When he was on earth, even Jesus called Satan the ruler of this world.

There has been and continues to be a war in heaven and on earth. Satan's battle has always been against God and Jesus Christ! Having lost the battle against Christ, Satan seeks to destroy God's family on earth, the church, because we are Christ's witnesses to the world. Read about the struggle with the beast in Daniel 7 and Revelation 12.

Satan hates God and would, if he could, pull him down from the throne of the universe. The threat and the presence of that hatred and determination in the universe will not be tolerated by God in the cease-less ages of eternity. God will absolutely destroy him because he has destroyed untold trillions and trillions of people through the ages of time. He is the source of untold misery, heartache, and bloodshed. Satan is the one ultimately responsible for causing the majority of the human family to be destroyed for eternity!

17 The LORD is righteous in all his ways
    and faithful in all he does.
18 The LORD is near to all who call on him,
    to all who call on him in truth.
19 He fulfills the desires of those who fear him;
    he hears their cry and saves them.
20 The LORD watches over all who love him,
    but all the wicked he will destroy. (Psalm 145:17-20).

Separated from God and Banned from the Tree of Life

In one of his many lessons, Billy Graham gave this illustration of that separation:

"The problem of Adam's sin reminds me of one of my summer vacations as a boy. My family was standing on the pristine shores of Jackson Lake, at the base of the Grand Teton Mountains in Wyoming. The reflection in the glassy calm waters of the lake perfectly mirrored the mountain range behind it. But the calm of the lake was disrupted when one of us boys took a small, flat stone and skipped it across the water's surface. In an instant, the image of the reflected peaks was distorted. The ripples seemed to wrinkle the entire lake. The likeness of my father and brothers in the once-smooth water was ruined. Adam's original sin in the garden was the pebble that shattered the calm with God, our Creator and Father.

So how can the problem be remedied? How can humanity's distorted lake be restored to its original peacefulness? Separation from God is everyone's problem, not just Adam's.

The Bible says, *"All have sinned and fall short of the glory of God"* (Romans 3:23).

Scripture plainly states, *"The wages of sin is death* (separation), *but the gift of God is eternal life in Christ Jesus our Lord."* (Romans 6:23). [3]

That sin exists does not undermine God's sovereignty nor omnipotence. My microscopic comprehension cannot fathom how God is bringing mankind to the perfection of the new creation, but I believe he is doing just that! I believe that *all things work together for good to those who love the Lord and have been called according to his purpose.* (Romans 8:28).

2

I AM WHO I AM

God's Message to His People Through Moses

When God spoke to Moses in the burning bush and gave him instructions for the Israelites,

¹³ Moses said to God, "Suppose I go to the Israelites and say to them, 'The God of your fathers has sent me to you,' and they ask me, 'What is his name?' Then what shall I tell them?"

¹⁴ God said to Moses, "I AM WHO I AM. This is what you are to say to the Israelites: 'I AM has sent me to you.'" ¹⁵ God also said to Moses, "Say to the Israelites, 'The LORD, the God of your fathers—the God of Abraham, the God of Isaac and the God of Jacob—has sent me to you.'

"This is my name forever, the name you shall call me from generation to generation. (Exodus 3:13-15).

Things We Can Only See by Faith

Can we explain how there can be God? Can we determine how He created something from nothing? Can we explain the workings of nature and the existence of man? We do not see heat nor cold, but we feel the influence of both. We do not see the wind nor understand electricity, but we know both exist. We know the effects of gravity because we can stand

9

firm when our feet hit the floor every morning. But trying to prove there
is a God is like striking a match to see the sun.

*[8] The wind blows wherever it pleases. You hear its sound, but you cannot
tell where it comes from or where it is going…* (John 3:8a).

So it is with God. We may not be able to explain, but *"The fool hath
said in his heart, there is no God."* (Psalm 14:1a).

See the Mighty Hand of God!

*As long as the earth endures, seedtime and harvest, cold and heat,
summer and winter, day and night will never cease.* (Genesis 8:22).

*He spreads out the northern skies over empty space; he suspends the
earth over nothing.* (Job 26:7).

*The heavens declare the glory of God; the skies proclaim the work of his
hands.* (Psalm 19:1).

*He makes grass grow for the cattle, and plants for people to culti-
vate— bringing forth food from the earth:* (Psalm 104:14).

*[4] He determines the number of the stars
    and calls them each by name.
[5] Great is our Lord and mighty in power;
    his understanding has no limit.
[6] The LORD sustains the humble
    but casts the wicked to the ground.*

*[7] Sing to the LORD with grateful praise;
    make music to our God on the harp.*

⁸ He covers the sky with clouds;
   he supplies the earth with rain
   and makes grass grow on the hills.
⁹ He provides food for the cattle
   and for the young ravens when they call.
(Psalm 147:4-9).

¹⁹By wisdom the Lᴏʀᴅ laid the earth's foundations, by understanding he set the heavens in place; ²⁰ by his knowledge the watery depths were divided, and the clouds let drop the dew. (Proverbs 3:19, 20).

This is what the Lᴏʀᴅ says,
he who appoints the sun
to shine by day,
who decrees the moon and stars
to shine by night,
who stirs up the sea
so that its waves roar—
the Lᴏʀᴅ Almighty is his name:
(Jeremiah 31:35).

Should you not fear me?" declares the Lord. Should you not tremble in my presence? I made the sand a boundary for the sea, an everlasting barrier it cannot cross. The waves may roll, but they cannot prevail; they may roar, but they cannot cross it. (Jeremiah 5:22).

Where were you when I laid the earth's foundation?
Tell me, if you understand. (Job 38:5).

   Yes, TELL ME IF YOU UNDERSTAND. This is what God commanded of Job. In other words, "Say so, if you know what it's all about!"
   It is impossible to adequately describe the greatness of God. There are absolutely no limits to His power. The puny mind of man cannot

fathom the infinity of God. If we could diligently study every truth available to us, we would still be grossly ignorant in the ways of God.

If all man's knowledge were combined, we would not be as wise as
God. God is not limited by time and space as are humans. Because he is
everywhere, he knows everything. There is nowhere in the universe that
you could be closer to God than you are right now. He hears your prayer
at the time he hears mine, and at the same time, he hears the prayers of
those on the other side of the world. He doesn't have to move from place
to place to hear our supplications because he is already there at the same
time he is here.

The following inadequate examples of trying to measure the power
of God may stimulate our understanding.

How High Can You Count?

Million is a word you probably hear every day, referring to lots of
things, ranging from city populations to your odds of winning the lot-
tery. It also appears in several colloquial phrases, such as *one in a million*
and *feeling like a million bucks!*

Next up is *billion*, which makes fewer cameos in our everyday
lives, though it still appears in discussions on finance and world population. Above that, *trillion* is reserved mostly for discussion of countries'
gross domestic product (GDP) and other macroeconomic topics. (Put
simply, GDP is a broad measurement of a nation's overall economic
activity).

Going even higher, we find ourselves in math and science territory,
where *quadrillion* is used to count things like photons, microorganisms,
and BTUs (traditional unit of heat; *defined* as the amount of heat required
to raise the temperature of one pound of water by one-degree Fahrenheit).

Higher still, quintillion is used to refer to the mass of the earth (in
tons) and the number of molecules in the human brain.[4]

There is no such thing as a highest possible number. No matter what
number you have, there is always a larger one. (For example, you could
always add 1 to your number to get a larger number).

The largest number that has a commonly-known specific name is a "googol," which is a 1 followed by a googol zeroes (1^{googol}), where a "googol" is larger than the number of elementary particles in the universe, which amount to only 10 to the 80th power. Later, another mathematician devised the term googolplex for 10 to the power of googol, that is, 1 followed by 10 to the power of 100 zeroes. The largest number that has a commonly-known specific name is a "googolplex," which is a 1 followed by a googol zeroes, where a "googol" is a 1 followed by 100 zeroes.

The mathematical question, "what is the highest possible number" has no answer, because there is no such thing. But the sociological question "what is the largest number that anyone has ever decided to give a specific name to, a name which has become commonly known" is, for now, a googolplex, until someone decides to coin a phrase for a still larger number, and it catches on and becomes commonly known. [5]

And now we have it…the gargoogolplex is a googolplex squared. Even if it were possible to measure an IQ of gargoogolplex; even a gargoogolplex squared, we would still not have an equivalent to the intelligence of God!

God is More Intelligent Than All People Who Ever Lived Combined!

An intelligence quotient (IQ) is a total score derived from several standardized tests designed to assess human intelligence. By this *definition*, approximately two-thirds of the population scores are between IQ 85 and IQ 115.

Let's take a look at people with the highest IQ ever recorded – the 10 most intelligent people of the world.

10. **Garry Kasparov** – alleged to have an IQ of 190, when he played to a draw against a chess computer that could calculate three million positions per second in 2003. He is a chess grandmaster from Russia. At the age of 22, he became the youngest undisputed world champion by defeating then-champion Anatoly Karpov

9. **Philip Emeagwali** - alleged to have an IQ of 190, is a Nigerian-born engineer, mathematician, computer scientist and geologist. He was one of two winners of the 1989 Gordon Bell Prize, a prize from the IEEE, for his use of a Connection Machine super-computer to help detect petroleum fields.

8. **Marilyn vos Savant** – verified IQ of 190 - popular columnist for Parade Magazine. Through "Ask Marilyn," readers can send puzzles and questions on different subjects for vos Savant to solve and answer.

7. **Mislav Predavec** - alleged to have an IQ of 192; Croatian math professor, president of the GenerIQ Society, an elite organization of some of the most intelligent people in the world. He is also the owner and director of a trade company.

6. **Rick Rosner** - alleged to have an IQ of 192; American television producer best known for creating the television show CHiPs. Rosner later developed a portable satellite television in partnership with DirecTV.

5. **Christopher Langan** - verified IQ of 195, reported to be between 195 and 210. He has been described as "the smartest man in America," as well as "the smartest man in the world" by the media. He began talking at six months. In addition, he taught himself to read when he was just 3 years old. Langan has developed a "theory of the relationship between mind and reality," which he calls the "Cognitive-Theoretic Model of the Universe" (CTMU).

4. **Dr. Evangelos Katsioulis** - alleged to have an IQ of 198 - Greek national who works as a medical doctor and psychiatrist. He has earned degrees in philosophy, medical research technology and psychopharmacology. He is the founder of the World Intelligence Network (WIN), an international organization of high IQ societies

3. **Kim Ung-Yong** - verified IQ of 210 - Korean civil engineer Ung Yong is considered the master in child prodigy. At the age of 6

months he was able to speak and understand Korean and other languages. At the age of 3 years, he could read several languages including; Korean, Japanese, German and English, as well as solve complex calculus problems as exposed live on Japanese television. He was listed in the Guinness Book of World Records under "Highest IQ."

1. **Terence Tao** - verified IQ of 230 - Australian-born Chinese American mathematician. He is working in harmonic analysis, partial differential equations, additive combinatorics, ergodic Ramsey theory, random matrix theory, and analytic number theory. At just 8 years, he achieved a score of 760 on the pre-1995 SAT, received a Ph.D from Princeton at 20 and at 24 became the youngest ever full professor at UCLA. [6]

Creative Genius!

Consider these people, who for centuries, have contributed to art, music, religion, philosophy, literature, movies, television, fiction, and animation of various subjects; who have views and visions that boggle our minds:

- Homer (750-650 BC)
- Plato (428-347 BC)
- Aristotle (384-322 BC)
- Michelangelo (1475-1564)
- Jane Austen (1787 to 1809)
- Beethoven (1770-1827)
- Sigmund Freud (1856 to 1939)
- Lewis Carroll (mid-to-late 1800's)
- Mozart (1756-1791)
- Copin (1810-1849)
- David Lipscomb (1831-1917)
- Marshall Keeble (1878-1968)
- Walt Disney (1901-1966)

- Stan Lee (1922-2018)
- Princess Diana (1961-1997)
- Dale Chihuly b. 1941
- George Lucas b. 1944
- Bill Gates b. 1955
- J. K. Rowling b. 1965
- And so many more…

Consider the Amazing Scenes We Have Experienced!

- Every fantastic movie that has ever been made
- Sunrise/sunset over the ocean
- Rockets into outer space
- Ski slopes in Aspen
- Northern lights in Iceland
- Helicopter rides over the Grand Canyon
- Disneyland and Disney World
- And so many more…

Seven Wonders of the Ancient World!

- Great Pyramid of Giza
- Hanging Gardens of Babylon
- Temple of Artemis at Ephesus
- Statue of Zeus at Olympia
- Mausoleum at Halicarnassus
- Colossus of Rhodes
- Lighthouse of Alexandria

Seven Wonders of the World in 2018!

- The Taj Mahal, India
- Christ the Redeemer, Brazil

- Petra, Jordan
- The Great Wall of China
- The Colosseum, Rome
- Machu Picchu, Peru
- Chichen Itza, Mexico

Some of the World's Most Beautiful Places!

- The iconic, pink-walled Palace of Winds in Jaipur, India where you can shop the jewelry district in the Amrapali Gem Palace for some of the world's rarest gems
- The Sagrada Familia church in Barcelona, Spain
- Edinburgh Castle in Scotland
- Tulips in Keukenhof Park, Holland, The Netherlands
- Hot-air balloons in Cappadocia, Turkey
- The serene beauty of the bamboo forest Arashiyama, Kyoto, Japan
- Salar de Uyuni, the reflective surface of the world's largest salt mine in Daniel Campos, Bolivia
- Bryce Canyon's layered red and orange rock pillars, known as *hoodoos in* Bryce, Utah USA
- Terraced rice fields in Mù Cang Chải, Vietnam
- The largest glacier in Vatnajökull, Iceland
- The lush Okavango Delta, Botswana is like a real-world Eden, where cheetahs, zebras, buffalo, and rhinos roam freely
- Cliffs of Moher, just south of Galway, Ireland, or you might know them better as the Cliffs of Insanity from the movie, *The Princess Bride*
- Benagil Sea Cave in Algarve, Portugal
- Ashikaga Flower Park in Japan, when wisteria trees bloom brilliantly for a few weeks every spring, turning the park into a vision of pastel pinks and purples

- Situated more than 8,000 feet above sea level, Kolukkumalai, Munnar, India is the highest tea estate in the world — and easily the most beautiful
- Known for its circular shape and strikingly deep blue color, the Great Blue Hole is a 1,000-foot-wide sinkhole in the middle of Belize's Lighthouse Reef
- Nā Pali Coast, Kauai, Hawaii one of the world's most insanely beautiful coastlines, which makes you work a bit to soak up its wonders — Nā Pali can only be seen from a helicopter, catamaran, or rather grueling hike
- Serengeti National Park, Tanzania
- The seemingly endless stretches of lavender fields make Provence, France one of the prettiest (and best-smelling) places in France
- Whether you're spotting the Northern Lights in Sweden or glaciers off the coast of Greenland, the Arctic Circle is a new kind of hidden paradise
- Glowworm Caves in Waitomo, New Zealand
- The stacked pools in Pamukkale are usually surrounded by snow and frozen waterfalls, but the blue waters are hot and open to bathers, Denizli, Turkey
- Victoria Falls, the largest waterfall in the world, that can be seen in southern Africa on the Zambezi River at the border between Zambia and Zimbabwe
- The otherworldly hues of the "Rainbow Mountains" Zhangye Danxia Geopark, China
- The famous 12 Apostle rock formations on Great Ocean Road, Australia
- Phi Phi Island in Ko Phi Phi Don, Thailand
- And so many more...

If you are not familiar with these places, look them up on the Internet and find amazing photographs. These are only small samples of the beauty of this earth. Not only did God create all of it, but he created the mind of mankind to be able to create even more beauty and adventure. Yet, I think that the intelligence and ability of these people, and beauty of these places are **rubble** compared to what he has in store for us in the new creation. I truly don't think we will ever be bored.

The point is that God's creation today is everywhere, doing everything to make our lives happy and meaningful.

However, the ungodly do not like to consider the power, knowledge and presence of God. They try in many ways to escape him. But we cannot escape; wherever we go, he is there. The infinity of God should be a source of comfort to his children. He is near when we need him, he knows our needs even before we do, and he can meet those needs.

Who can hide in secret places so that I cannot see them? declares the LORD. "Do not I fill heaven and earth? declares the LORD. (Jeremiah 23:24).

Jesus looked at them and said, "With man this is impossible, but with God all things are possible." (Matthew 19:26).

[27] God did this so that they would seek him and perhaps reach out for him and find him, though he is not far from any one of us. [28] 'For in him we live and move and have our being.' (Acts 17:27, 28a).

Things We Think We Own, but We Don't

Absolutely nothing you own is really yours! Absolutely nothing I own is really mine! We have been given many physical blessings and material goods; but as it has been said many times, we brought nothing into this world, and it is certain we will take nothing out. You might say that God has loaned them to us for a while and the joy or sorrow, the laughter or tears involved in the using are just interest on the loan.

With whatever we have been given to use, there is also a responsibility to use it to the glory of God. The most important physical possession we have been given is our body, for within our bodies exists the only part of us that will live forever… our soul.

19

*To the L*ORD *your God belong the heavens, even the highest heavens, the earth and everything in it.* (Deuteronomy 10:14).

⁵Now if you obey me fully and keep my covenant, then out of all nations you will be my treasured possess-ion. Although the whole earth is mine, ⁶you will be for me a kingdom of priests and a holy nation. (Exodus 19:5, 6).

I have no need of a bull from your stall or of goats from your pens, ¹⁰for every animal of the forest is mine, and the cattle on a thousand hills. ¹¹I know every bird in the mountains, and the insects in the fields are mine. ¹²If I were hungry, I would not tell you, for the world is mine, and all that is in it. (Said the Lord: Psalm 50:10·12).

*'The silver is mine and the gold is mine,' declares the L*ORD *Almighty.* (Haggai 2:8).

For everyone belongs to me, the parent as well as the child—both alike belong to me. (Ezekiel 18:4a).

That is why Paul said in Romans 12:1, *"Therefore, I urge you, brothers and sisters, in view of God's mercy, to offer your bodies as a living sac-rifice, holy and pleasing to God—this is your true and proper worship."*

⁷For none of us lives for ourselves alone, and none of us dies for our-selves alone. ⁸If we live, we live for the Lord; and if we die, we die for the Lord. So, whether we live or die, we belong to the Lord. ⁹For this very reason, Christ died and returned to life so that he might be the Lord of both the dead and the living. (Romans 14:7-9).

¹⁹Do you not know that your bodies are temples of the Holy Spirit, who is in you, whom you have received from God? You are not your own; ²⁰you were bought at a price. Therefore, honor God with your bodies. (1 Corinthians 6:19-20).

Solomon tells us that the fear of the Lord is the beginning of knowledge (Proverbs 1:7). When we attain a healthy respect and recognition of the complete superiority and infinity of God and understand that our total existence belongs to him, we should have the desire to get acquainted with God through his word; and as we open our eyes to behold his splendid creation, we will see the word of God confirmed by his wondrous works.

3

THE BIBLE, OUR STANDARD FOR LIFE AND DEATH

The Double-Edged Sword

Researchers have found that **the Bible** far outsold any other book, with a whopping 3.9 billion copies sold over the last 50 years. That's a lot of Bibles!

There is just something about a Bible --

The writer of the letter to the Hebrews said, "*For the word of God is alive and active. Sharper than any **double-edged sword**, it penetrates even to dividing soul and spirit, joints and marrow; it judges the thoughts and attitudes of the heart.*" (Hebrews 4:12).

John's Revelation describes how John saw Jesus: "*In his right hand he held seven stars, and coming out of his mouth was a sharp, **double-edged sword**. His face was like the sun shining in all its brilliance.*" (Revelation 1:16).

"*To the angel of the church in Pergamum write: These are the words of him who has the sharp, **double-edged sword**.*" (Revelation 2:12).

"The Word of God" is clearly defined as Jesus in John chapter 1.

Have you noticed that when this metaphor was translated into the various translations, "Word," capitalized, is defined as Jesus Christ? In the various translations, "God's word" is lower case "word" and is defined as God's message to mankind, the book we know as the Bible. For example,

*Do your best to present yourself to God as one approved, a worker who does not need to be ashamed and who correctly handles the **word of truth**.* (2 Timothy 2:15).

*In fact, though by this time you ought to be teachers, you need someone to teach you the elementary truths of **God's word** all over again. You need milk, not solid food!* (Hebrews 5:12).

The same is true of the use of the word "sword." Paul gave a metaphor in Ephesians 6:17, describing the warfare in which Christians are engaged against the devil. He said to use the **sword** of the Spirit, which is the **word** of God.

*[11] Put on the full armor of God, so that you can take your stand against the devil's schemes. [12] For our struggle is not against flesh and blood, but against the rulers, against the authorities, against the powers of this dark world and against the spiritual forces of evil in the heavenly realms -- [17] Take the helmet of salvation and the **sword** of the Spirit, which is the **word** of God.* (Ephesians 6:11-12, 17).

> *"First, the Word of God, which is to be our one weapon, is of noble origin; for it is the sword of the Spirit. It has the properties of a sword, and those were given it by the Spirit of God.*
> *"Here we note that the Holy Spirit has a sword. He is quiet as the dew, tender as the anointing oil, soft as the zephyr of eventide, and peaceful as a dove; and yet, under another aspect, he wields a deadly weapon. He*

is the Spirit of judgment and the Spirit of burning, and
he beareth not the sword in vain. Of him it may be said,
"The Lord is a man of war: Jehovah is his name." --
Charles Spurgeon [7]

Therefore, the metaphor of the **double-edged sword** carries much more significance when you realize that it describes the word of God as a sword that cuts both ways. It can be a blessing, and it can be a judgment.

The Bible is Precious!

My grandmother taught me that the Bible is precious! She loved the word "precious" and often said she would love to hear a sermon describing the meaning of the word precious. I don't think she ever heard that sermon, but nevertheless, the Bible is a precious book!

This is true even though there have been many who disbelieve, criticize and condemn it as fiction. Some deny that the Bible is anything but a fine work of literature; some say the existence of Jehovah, God of hosts, is only in the minds of weak men and women who need something to lean on. But the fact is, if it is not true, if it is only fiction, it is not a fine work of literature, it is a lie... all of it! Then we are most miserable and hopeless.

Truly, it is our standard for life and death and the source of our knowledge and hope. At least let us give it the benefit of the doubt.

For many years now, the atheistic theory of the evolution of earth and man has permeated our society to the extent that schools have been encouraged, and at times required, to teach this theory in preference to and in place of the account of the divine creation as recorded in Genesis.

However, the recent recommendation of leading educators to stress to students that evolution is just a theory and that the Bible account of the creation should also be taught in schools is encouraging. Some educators, it would seem, are beginning to realize that the Bible, if studied, is highly compatible with science and relates information about our universe that it has taken mankind many centuries to discover in other ways.

The contents of the Bible need only to be investigated for one to obtain the answers to questions regarding the existence and nature of God and spiritual matters. It is to this book we will turn in this and following lessons to see if we can gain more understanding about God's plan for us to spend eternity with him in heaven. [8]

The good thing is that he has given us some really great information so that we don't have to blindly speculate. By divine revelation, we have some solid data to make us more sighted. It is up to us to believe it or not, but wouldn't it be a shame to take that information and hide it in the ground or be indifferent about it like the servant who hid his master's gold in the ground? (Matthew 25:24-26).

Has anyone ever challenged you about your faith that God is alive and well in heaven and overseeing everything that is happening here right now?

Tell them that you have a friend, Jesus, who came down to tell us about it. He said, *"I am the way and the truth and the life. No one comes to the Father except through me."* (John 14:6).

We may be wise in all aspects of life and education, but without a knowledge of the Bible, we are ignorant. There are so many people in the world who are searching for truth, and many stumble over the very source to which they can go to find the answers to their questions. Let us not form an opinion that discredits the scriptures without investigating them. Give the Bible a chance. It is inexhaustible in content. The more you study it, the more you want to study it; the more you learn, the more you realize how much there is to learn from it. The more familiar you become with it, the more you will love it; because it truly is precious! [9]

Open Your Bible

When we first open the Bible, there are so many words on so many pages, we may tend to immediately become discouraged with the density of it. Where do we begin to try to understand its contents?

Dispensational Bible Study

First, let's get acquainted with the layout. This manner of Bible study is "dispensational" in contrast to a "Christocentric" approach to study, which we will also look at. For a new student of the Bible, the understanding that can be acquired by way of dispensational Bible study is a good place to begin.

The Bible is a volume of sixty-six "books," a combination of two parts, the Old Testament and the New Testament. Each of the books are divided into chapters and verses. Although the original manuscripts were not so divided, devoted translators made those divisions to assist us in studying the scriptures. And it does help, usually, although the chapters sometimes break thoughts that may be continued in the next chapter.

The Old Testament contains thirty-nine books that tell the story of the Hebrew Nation.

Genesis–Esther	History	17 books
Job–Song of Solomon	Poetry	5 books
Isaiah–Malachi	Prophecy	17 books

The New Testament contains twenty-seven books that tell of the MAN whom that Nation produced. It's all about Jesus!

Matthew–John	Biography	4 books
Acts of the Apostles	History	1 book
Romans–Jude	Letters	21 books
Revelation	Prophecy	1 book

Ask Four Questions

When reading any portion of the Bible, it is important to determine the answers to four questions.

1. Who is speaking?
2. To whom is it spoken?
3. For what purpose is it spoken?

4. When was it spoken?

For example, in Genesis 6:14, *[13] So God said to Noah, "I am going to put an end to all people, for the earth is filled with violence because of them. I am surely going to destroy both them and the earth. [14] So make yourself an ark of cypress wood; make rooms in it and coat it with pitch inside and out. [15] This is how you are to build it...* (Genesis 6:13-15a).

We see why God chose Noah for this task from the previous verses. He was a righteous man and God wanted to save him and his family from the coming destruction; but we understand that God is not telling *us* to build an ark.

Three Types of Passages

Breaking it down into very simple types of writing, there are at least three kinds of passages in the Bible.

1. **Narrative** – These are passages that simply relate the amazing things that happened in the Bible such as Genesis describing God's creation of heaven and earth, or Jonah being swallowed by a big fish.
2. **Prophecy** – These passages of prophecy and revelation brought attention to what events would come to pass and why.
3. **Commands** – These instructions that were given directly by God, or given by his Spirit to his appointed messengers, who would in turn give those instructions to the recipients of the message. God always expected obedience...he still does.

Three Types of Commands

1. When one is told to do something in no uncertain terms, that is a ***direct command***, such as Acts 2:38, *"Repent and be baptized,*

every one of you, in the name of Jesus Christ for the forgiveness of your sins. And you will receive the gift of the Holy Spirit.

2. By **example**, we see that the disciples *"continued steadfastly in the apostles' doctrine and fellowship, and in breaking of bread, and in prayers."* (Acts 2:42).

3. A lesser used method of teaching is sometimes called **necessary inference**. To illustrate, when Philip preached to the Ethiopian eunuch, he told him about Jesus, and the eunuch wanted to be baptized. Philip's teaching obviously included the need to be baptized.

[34] The Ethiopian eunuch asked Philip, *"Tell me, please, who is the prophet talking about, himself or someone else?"* [35] *Then Philip began with that very passage of Scripture and told him the good news about Jesus.*

[36] *As they traveled along the road, they came to some water and the eunuch said, "Look, here is water. What can stand in the way of my being baptized?"* [37] *Philip said, "If you believe with all your heart, you may." The eunuch answered, "I believe that Jesus Christ is the Son of God."* [38] *And he gave orders to stop the chariot. Then both Philip and the eunuch went down into the water and Philip baptized him.* (Acts 8:34-39).

Additionally, there are passages that are **figurative**; such as Jesus referring to himself as a door (John 10:9), and as the vine (John 15:1), as the bread of life (John 6:35). He used these illustrations to convey to us some ideas of his nature. Usually, figurative language uses words, experiences, and things with which we are familiar to describe an idea that is unfamiliar to us.

Other passages are to be taken **literally**. For example, when Jesus was asked, [36] *"Teacher, which is the greatest commandment in the Law?"* [37] *Jesus replied: "'Love the Lord your God with all your heart and with all your soul and with all your mind.'* [38] *This is the first and greatest* *commandment.* [39] *And the second is like it: 'Love your neighbor as your-self.'* (Matthew 22:36-39), there is no mistake that he meant it literally.

We should be careful not to take a literal passage and try to make figurative, nor try to make a figurative passage into a literal one. If it gives you trouble at first, don't be discouraged; it gets easier with practice.

Three Dispensations

God has used different methods of instructions to his people depending on the period of time in which an individual lived or lives.

There have been three distinct ages or dispensations since the beginning of time. Under the ***Patriarchal Dispensation***, there was no formal worship as we know it. There was no written law and no specific house of worship. God spoke directly to the father (patriarch) of each family and often used dreams, visions, and angels to convey his messages. This dispensation lasted approximately 2,500 years, from Adam to the giving of the Law to Moses on Mt. Sinai.

During the ***Mosaical Dispensation***, the law that God gave through Moses was in force. This was a special law for special people, the descendants of Abraham, through whom God had promised that all the nations of the earth would be blessed (Genesis 22:18). This nation became known as the Israelites, or Jews, and the Law was given only to them. This dispensation lasted about 1,500 years, from the giving of the Law to Moses on Mt. Sinai to the death of Jesus Christ, who by his death fulfilled the Law and took it out of the way, nailing it to his cross. (Colossians 2:14).

Understanding these distinctions can be confusing to religious people today. The truth is that Jews are no longer subject to the Law of Moses, although many traditions are still observed. Gentiles were never subject to that law, and all nations are now living under the law of Christ, his last will and testament, the New Testament, which was sealed by his death (Hebrews 9:15-17). This is the fulfillment of God's promise to Abraham that through his seed all nations of the earth would be blessed.

This ***Christian Dispensation*** has now been in existence almost 2,000 years and will remain so until Christ comes again to receive his disciples and present them to his Father in heaven. It is to this Christ we must listen now, because it is by him that God speaks to us. (Matthew 17:5; Hebrews 1:1).

This does not mean that the Old Testament is of no importance to us. To the contrary, reading the Old Testament is helpful to a good understanding of the New.

15 Do your best to present yourself to God as one approved, a worker who does not need to be ashamed and who correctly handles the word of truth. (2 Timothy 2:15).

There are many helps available to use while you study to learn. Reach out to resources like the Internet, dictionaries, concordances, commentaries, and different translations of the Bible for assistance on your journey into God's word.

Christocentric Bible Study

This is not an either/or question for me. I think both dispensational and Christocentric Bible studies have merit.

16 For God so loved the world that he gave his one and only Son, that whoever believes in him shall not perish but have eternal life. 17 For God did not send his Son into the world to condemn the world, but to save the world through him. (John 3:16, 17).

In Jesus Christ, God has revealed Himself as completely as it is possible to reveal Himself in a human life. Jesus is the express image of God's person and when we see and know him, we see and know the Father. This being true, then we should treat Jesus as the means by which we get to know God the Father. Our approach to the understanding of God, Christ, and the church must then be Christocentric, and everything in the Old Testament will have undertones and futuristic projections to

31

the Christ child and his ultimate crucifixion, resurrection, the coming of the Holy Spirit, and the establishment of the church.

The Church in the Power of the Spirit by Jürgen Moltmann, is a "contribution to messianic ecclesiology," an exploration into what the church is and why the church exists.

The entire theme of his theological insight centers on the idea of there being an expressly intimate connection between Christ and the church. The church is not only believing in and pointing towards the risen Christ, the church has Christ as the foundation of its entire being. Moltmann writes, "Every statement about the church will be a statement about Christ. Every statement about Christ also implies a statement about the church."[10]

This doesn't mean that we should read or speak about only resurrection texts or texts about the church, but it should mean that we work at seeing how all other texts enable us to understand the cross of Christ so that it will in turn open our eyes to everything else. This means that our study habits and approaches should work to get to know Christ. For example, when Paul was describing the resurrected body to the church in Corinth, we can see Christ in Adam. (1 Corinthians 15:25-57).

Perhaps one of the greatest messages that Isaiah prophetically speaks about Jesus the Messiah is the redemptive nature of his gospel. Isaiah speaks of the sin that Jesus would bear for many. This helps us to know and understand that the life, death, and resurrection of Jesus ultimately redeems us into a right relationship with God. You and I today can have the peace of God because he *"poured out his soul to death."*

We do not deserve this redemption. However, according to Titus, God's grace has appeared to us bringing salvation through Jesus. The grace of God allows for this redemption through Jesus for sinners like you and me. As we preach the prophetic gospel of Jesus in Isaiah, we must make it known to our audience that God's ever forward plan for the redemption of mankind is found in this passage pointing us to the coming Messiah Jesus, our redeemer.

The story of Jesus doesn't simply begin in the stable in Bethlehem. This story has been in motion since before the foundation of the world. The Jesus that Isaiah so faithfully proclaimed hundreds of years before his birth would ultimately be the hope of the world! In fact, as you read the Bible you will come to know Jesus as the main character in the ever-advancing story of the grace of God. As we preach Jesus, let us tell the whole story. Taking the example of the evangelist Philip, let's start with the Old Testament. [11]

4

THE UNWORLDLY
KINGDOM OF GOD

Promise to Abraham

It appears that God, in his omniscience, knew humanity would sin, bringing separation between them and himself, and he put his plan into action to bring about a reconciliation through his Son (Genesis 3:15; Acts 2:23).

As we see history unfolding by reading Genesis in the Old Testament, we see that Abram, later to be named Abraham, was given a promise that through him all the nations of the earth would be blessed. Read this history in the book of Genesis. The plan began to take shape when God made that promise to Abraham that his descendants would be as numerous as the stars in the sky and as the sand on the seashore, that they would be a great nation, and that through Abraham's descendants all nations on the earth would be blessed because of his obedience (Genesis 22:16-18).

Abraham was the father of Ishmael and Isaac; Isaac was the son of promise and father of Jacob and Esau. Jacob had twelve sons and one daughter. Jacob, later to be named Israel, and his twelve sons were the beginning of the Jewish nation, which also came to be known as Israel—the seed that would bring the promised Messiah through Jacob's son, Judah.

Read Genesis 12:1-3; 18:18, 19; Numbers 24:17, 19; Deuteronomy 18:15; Isaiah 11:1-5, 10-12; 42:1; 49:5-12; Jeremiah 23:5; 33:15.

God's Kingdom Has Always Been

God's kingdom is. It has always been. It has stretched from the beginning of time as we know it and will be throughout eternity. But it has not always been structured on earth as an existent form of religious organization.

The word kingdom is capable of three different meanings: (1) the realm over which a monarch reigns, (2) the people over whom he or she reigns, and (3) the actual reign or rule itself. All three meanings are found in the New Testament. The kingdom of God is sometimes referring to the people of the kingdom (Revelation 1:6; 5:10). The kingdom of God is the realm in which God's reign is experienced.

Israel, God's chosen people, was set apart for a covenant relationship with God. It is universally recognized that Israel was a singular community. From the beginning of its existence as a nation, it bore the character of a religious and moral community. A theocratic commonwealth, having Jehovah himself as the head and ruler. The theocracy supplied the centralizing power, constituting Israel a nation. In lieu of a strong political center, the common faith in him, the God of Israel, kept the tribes together. The consciousness that Jehovah was Israel's king was deeply rooted. Read Exodus 15:18; 19:6.

Jehovah's kingship is evidenced by the laws he gave to Israel to and through Moses, by the fact that justice was administered in his name (Exodus 22:28), and by his leading and aiding Israel in its wars. (Exodus 14:13,14; 15:3).

Israel, God's chosen family, frequently disappointed God, but never ended his love for them. Over and over, historically and biblically, we see God's plan to redeem his family because ultimately, he wanted to bring them back to himself.

The pattern that is seen repeatedly in the Old Testament was that the Israelites forgot God and he would give them over to be oppressed by other nations. Then they would cry out to the Lord and he would send them a deliverer. The period of the Judges lasted about 300 years. They had no king, but everyone did as they saw fit.

Not until the time of the prophet, Samuel, was a formal, earthly kingdom established over Israel. At first Samuel resisted, but God directed Samuel to give them a king -- since the introduction of a kingship typifying the kingship of Christ lay within the parameters of his plan -- not according to their desire, but in accordance with the instructions of the law concerning kings (Deuteronomy 17:14-20) to safeguard their liberties and prevent the forfeiture of their mission.

The King of Israel was not a constitutional monarch in the modern sense; he was responsible to Jehovah, who had chosen him. His kingship in relation to Jehovah, who was Israel's true king, implied that he was Jehovah's servant and his earthly substitute. Saul was Israel's first king. Read 1 Samuel 9 and 10.

After a forty-two-year reign, God was grieved that he had made Saul king over Israel because of his disobedience. Saul died because he was unfaithful to the Lord; he did not keep the work of the Lord, even consulting a medium for guidance, and did not inquire of the Lord. So the Lord turned the kingdom over to David, son of Jesse. (1 Samuel 16:1-13; 1 Chronicles 10:13, 14).

King David appeared as the type of king in whom the divine ideal of a king was to find its perfect realization. After David and Solomon, the kingdom became divided, logistically, and religiously. The loss of reverence for God, idolatry, and evil intent plagued the nations. Israel's kingdom terminated in the Babylonian exile, and it remains to be said only that the final attempt of Israel in its revolt against the Roman Empire to establish the old monarchy, resulted in its downfall as a nation, because it would not learn the lesson that the future of a nation does not depend upon political greatness, but upon the fulfillment of its divine mission. [12]

Israel's great hope to restore their kingdom to power was believed to be imminent through the promised Messiah. We know, however, that the Jews expected a structured kingdom, marked by pomp and state; a kingdom on the lines of David's or Solomon's kingdoms. Israel was looking for an earthly, physical kingdom and an earthly, physical king. But listen to the prophets:

"In the time of those kings (the kings in Nebuchadnezzar's dream) the God of heaven will set up a kingdom that will never be destroyed, nor will it be left to another people. It will crush all those kingdoms and bring them to an end, but it will itself endure forever." Daniel 2:44. (Parentheses mine. SM).

Read Daniel 7:13, 14 and Micah 5:2.

Bethlehem -- sometimes referred to as the city of David; the birthplace of Jesus. (1 Samuel 16:1; Micah 5:2; Matthew 2:5, 6; Luke 2:11). The key to Israel's future was a coming leader... a very unusual leader. People naturally expected the Messiah to be a triumphant warrior, especially since many Old Testament prophecies spoke of him that way. But this king would come on a donkey instead of a war-horse (Zechariah 9:9; Matthew 21:5).

Zechariah speaks of a shepherd... a term for "leader," who would be rejected by the nation (Zechariah 11:4-17). It describes a nation in mourning for *"the one they have pierced"* (Zechariah 12:10). All these predictions of a coming leader were quoted in the New Testament as applying to Jesus: a king without an army, whose crown was made of thorns.

In all the Old Testament, only Isaiah (especially in chapter 53) captures so fully the paradox of Jesus' life: gentle leadership that triumphs through suffering.[13]

The fulfillment of prophecy through a humble carpenter did not fit Israel's image of the coming Messiah so he was rejected. There can be no question that Christ is set before us in scripture as a king. The very name Christ or Messiah suggests kingship.   The scriptures plainly declare, and Christ himself clearly taught, that his kingship was spiritual. *"My kingdom,"* he said, *"is not of this world."* (John 3:3-5; 18:36). He adds, *"If my kingdom were of this world, then would my servants fight, that I should not be delivered to the Jews."*

38

Because it is of an unworldly origin, it is not to be propagated by worldly means, and the non-use of worldly means declares its essential spirituality, to be of an unworldly character -- its otherworldliness. [14]

A Kingdom for All Nations [15]

In the Old Testament, God's kingdom on earth was for Israel alone. Just as the law that God gave to Moses was for Israel alone. But the prophets spoke of a time when Israel would see God's kingdom on earth come with power and that ALL nations would be drawn to it. (Remember... a spiritual kingdom). And these things would come to pass with miracles, wonders and signs. The Lord's kingdom was prophesied in the Old Testament. (Psalm 69:35; Daniel 2:44; 7:13, 14; Isaiah 2:2, 3; 9:6,7; Joel 2:28-32; Micah 4:1, 2.). Listen to the prophet Isaiah:

*"In the last days the mountain of the Lord's temple will be established as chief among the mountains; it will be raised above the hills, and **all nations** will stream to it. Many peoples will come and say, 'Come, let us go up to the mountain of the Lord, to the house of the God of Jacob. He will teach us his ways so that we may walk in his paths.' The law will go out from Zion, the word of the Lord from Jerusalem."* (Isaiah 2:2-3).

Isaiah's prophecy was fulfilled on the day of Pentecost in Jerusalem as recorded in Acts 2. The New Testament "gospels" (although there is only one gospel written by four different men, Matthew, Mark, Luke and John), tell the good news of Jesus. They each include portions of the biography of the Son of God and man. In them we see the kingdom being close at hand. The plan was close to fruition and preparation was being made for it.

Read Matthew 3:1,2; 12:28; 16:16-19; Mark 9:1; Luke 16:16; 24:44-49; Acts 1:1-8.

"I tell you the truth, some who are standing here will not taste death before they see the kingdom of God come with power." (Mark 9:1).

Either the earthly form of the unworldly kingdom has already been established, or there are some very old people still waiting for it to come.

God's love for his people, his kingdom, the church, is alive and well, NOW.

John Calvin said it is the task of the church to make the kingdom visible. We do that by living in such a way that we bear witness to the reality of the kingship of Christ in our jobs, our families, our schools, and even our checkbooks, because God in Christ is King over every one of these spheres of life. The only way the kingdom of God is going to be manifest in this world before Christ comes is if we manifest it by the way we live as citizens of heaven and subjects of the King.

5

HEAVEN CAME DOWN AND GLORY FILLED MY SOUL

O what a wonderful, wonderful day,
Day I will never forget;
After I'd wandered in darkness away,
Jesus my Savior I met.
O what a tender, compassionate friend,
He met the need of my heart;
Shadows dispelling, with joy I am telling,
He made all the darkness depart.
Heaven came down and glory filled my soul,
When at the cross the Savior made me whole;
My sins were washed away
And my night was turned to day,
Heaven came down and glory filled my soul!
Now I've a hope that will surely endure
After the passing of time;
I have a future in heaven for sure
There in those mansions sublime.
And it's because of that wonderful day,
When at the cross I believed;
Riches eternal and blessings supernal,
From His precious hand I received.

Heaven came down and glory filled my soul,
When at the cross the Savior made me whole;
My sins were washed away
And my night was turned to day,
Heaven came down and glory filled my soul!

© 1961 John W. Peterson Music Company.
All rights reserved. Used by permission

The Time That Would Come, The One Who Would Come, Jesus Christ

*³⁸ For I have **come down from heaven** not to do my will but to do the will of him who sent me. ³⁹ And this is the will of him who sent me, that I shall lose none of all those he has given me, but raise them up at the last day. ⁴⁰ For my Father's will is that everyone who looks to the Son and believes in him shall have eternal life, and I will raise them up at the last day.*

⁴¹ At this the Jews there began to grumble about him because he said, "I am the bread that came down from heaven." ⁴² They said, "Is this not Jesus, the son of Joseph, whose father and mother we know? How can he now say, 'I came down from heaven?'"

⁵⁰ But here is the bread that comes down from heaven, which anyone may eat and not die. ⁵¹ I am the living bread that came down from heaven. Whoever eats this bread will live forever. This bread is my flesh, which I will give for the life of the world." (John 6:38-42, 50).

To Restore Us to Holiness

The great object of the prophecies of the Old Testament was to unfold the redemptive plan for mankind. Sir Isaac Watts said, "It is the great design of the gospel to restore us to holiness as well as happiness."

Most of the Old Testament is devoted to the story of the nation chosen by God through whom the redeemer would come into the world. The New Testament is devoted to the story of the man that nation produced and how his life, death and resurrection gives hope to sinful humanity through his kingdom. The resurrection of Jesus Christ ended the separation from God that sin brought into the world and has brought God and man back together.

Jesus told his apostles that he would die but would be raised from the dead after three days, and after his resurrection he was going to send them the Spirit of truth, which the Father had promised them (John 15:26; 16:13), and they would be baptized with the Holy Spirit. Read Matthew 3:1, 2, 11; 12:28; 16:16-19; Mark 9:1; Luke 24; John 3:3-8.

Before Jesus left his disciples, he promised them that they would not be alone and helpless in the world. He said that after he was gone, he would send them a helper, a teacher, a comforter to sustain and assist them in carrying out the church's mission.

He called this helper the Holy Spirit. It would be the Holy Spirit's purpose to *"guide them into all truth"* and to remind the apostles of all that Jesus had said and done. He instructed them to wait in Jerusalem until they had been clothed with power from on high (Luke 24:49).

"When the Counselor comes, whom I will send to you from the Father, the Spirit of truth who goes out from the Father, he will testify about me. And you also must testify, for you have been with me from the beginning." (John 15:26).

"But you will receive power when the Holy Spirit comes on you; and you will be my witnesses in Jerusalem, and in all Judea and Samaria, and to the ends of the earth." (Acts 1:8).

The Coming of the Holy Spirit

Read Matthew 3:11; Mark 1:8; Luke 3:16; John 1:33; Acts 1:4,5; 2:1-4; 10:44-47; 11:15-17.

All the prophecies and promises came to fruition as recorded in the second chapter of Acts. It was in Jerusalem approximately AD 33 where the apostles were waiting, just as Jesus had told them to wait, on the day of Pentecost that the apostles were baptized with the Holy Spirit. Characteristics of this manifestation on that day were that the Spirit's coming was visible in the tongues of fire, and audible in the sound of a rushing, violent wind. They were immersed in the Holy Spirit -- they were overwhelmed with the Holy Spirit. The results were that they were empowered to speak the good news of the Lord and do everything necessary to confirm that message. Here is where we first read of the church being in existence. Never before that time was the church spoken of as being in existence and never after that was it spoken of as being in the future.

It was on that day that repentance and remission of sins were preached in the name of Jesus for the first time. (Luke 24:47; Acts 2:38).

But not only that. In Acts 2:16, Peter, explaining to the audience the events they were witnessing that day, said *"This is what was spoken by the prophet Joel."*

They were witnessing the fulfillment of Joel's prophecy that the Spirit of God would be poured out upon all flesh, Jew and Gentile; men and women. Joel lived in a time when only Jews were in a covenant relationship with God. Gentiles were not part of the covenant, but his prophecy spoke of a time when Jews and Gentiles both would be in a covenant relationship with God. (Acts 2:17,18).

In Paul's letter to the church in Ephesus, he explained to them how Christ had come to make **one new man out of two.** By abolishing the law of Moses with its commandments and regulations, He brought the Jews and the Gentiles into reconciliation with God through His death on the cross.

"He came and preached peace to you who were far away (Gentiles) *and peace to those who were near* (Jews). *For through him we both have access to the Father by one Spirit. Consequently, you* (Gentiles) *are no longer foreigners and aliens, but fellow citizens with God's people* (Jews) *and members of God's household, built on the foundation of the apostles and prophets, with Christ Jesus himself as the chief corner-stone. In him the whole building is joined together and rises to become a holy temple in the Lord. And in him you too are being built together to become a dwelling in which God lives by his Spirit."* (Ephesians 2:17-22, Parentheses mine. SM).

But not only that. These occurrences on the day of Pentecost were also the fulfillment of the promise that Jesus gave his apostles that they would receive power when the Holy Spirit came on them, that they would be his witnesses in Jerusalem and in all Judea and Samaria, and to the ends of the earth.

It was more than twelve men being the focal point in a crowd of Jews. It was more than their ability to speak in languages they had never learned. It was more than Peter telling the good news of salvation to the people who had crucified Jesus. It was even more than they could comprehend. It was the fulfillment of God's promise that Israel would be restored to their kingdom.

But many misunderstood. Even after Jesus was resurrected, they were still saying, *"Lord, are you at this time going to restore the kingdom to Israel?"* (Acts 1:6).

Even though Jesus had tried to tell them that his kingdom was not of this world, they still did not understand that it was a spiritual kingdom with Christ their Messiah and king, who was bringing spiritual salvation to **every nation**, not just Israel, and that he was reigning at the right hand of God. But Jesus patiently told them that when the Holy Spirit came on them, they would be his witnesses in Jerusalem, in Judea and Samaria, and to the ends of the earth (Acts 1:7, 8).

The Holy Spirit is Our Guarantee of Salvation

The Holy Spirit – the part of God that he has given to each member of his family.

Peter, on the day of Pentecost, told his audience of Jewish believers that they would receive the gift of the Holy Spirit when they were baptized. (Acts 2:38-39; Acts 5:30-32).

[21] Now it is God who makes both us and you stand firm in Christ. He anointed us, [22] set his seal of ownership on us, and put his Spirit in our hearts as a deposit, guaranteeing what is to come. (2 Corinthians 1:21-22).

[4] For while we are in this tent, we groan and are burdened, because we do not wish to be unclothed but to be clothed instead with our heavenly dwelling, so that what is mortal may be swallowed up by life. [5] Now the one who has fashioned us for this very purpose is God, who has given us the Spirit as a deposit, guaranteeing what is to come. (2 Corinthians 5:4-5).

[13] And you also were included in Christ when you heard the message of truth, the gospel of your salvation. When you believed, you were marked in him with a seal, the promised Holy Spirit, [14] who is a deposit guaranteeing our inheritance until the redemption of those who are God's possession—to the praise of his glory. (Ephesians 1:13-14).

All people, all nations, are guaranteed salvation through Christ, because God has given us his Spirit. Not because WE can make good the guarantee, but because GOD can and will make good the guarantee! He owns us!

The First Gentile, Cornelius, Became Part of the Family of God

The apostle, Peter, who prominently spoke to the Jews on the day of Pentecost, was given the task of teaching a Gentile Centurion, Cornelius, about the Lord Jesus.

If you know anything about Bibly history, you remember that Gentiles were considered unworthy of being in God's family. Only Israelites were counted as part of God's covenant. But Jesus changed all that!

*7 While talking with him, Peter went inside and found a large gathering of people. ²⁸ He said to them: "You are well aware that it is against our law for a Jew to associate with or visit a Gentile. But God has shown me that **I should not call anyone impure or unclean**. ²⁹ So when I was sent for, I came without raising any objection. May I ask why you sent for me?"*

³⁰ Cornelius answered: "Three days ago I was in my house praying at this hour, at three in the afternoon. Suddenly a man in shining clothes stood before me ³¹ and said, 'Cornelius, God has heard your prayer and remembered your gifts to the poor. ³² Send to Joppa for Simon who is called Peter. He is a guest in the home of Simon the tanner, who lives by the sea.' ³³ So I sent for you immediately, and it was good of you to come. Now we are all here in the presence of God to listen to everything the Lord has commanded you to tell us."

*³⁴ Then Peter began to speak: "I now realize how true it is that **God does not show favoritism ³⁵ but accepts from every nation the one who fears him and does what is right.** ³⁶ You know the message God sent to the people of Israel, announcing the good news of peace through Jesus Christ, who is Lord of all. ³⁷ You know what has happened throughout the province of Judea, beginning in Galilee after the baptism that John preached— ³⁸ how God anointed Jesus of Nazareth with the Holy Spirit and power, and how he went around doing good and healing all who were under the power of the devil, because God was with him.*

³⁹ "We are witnesses of everything he did in the country of the Jews and in Jerusalem. They killed him by hanging him on a cross, ⁴⁰ but God raised him from the dead on the third day and caused him to be seen.⁴¹ He was not seen by all the people, but by witnesses whom God had already chosen—by us who ate and drank with him after he rose from the dead. [42] He commanded us to preach to the people and to testify that he is the one whom God appointed as judge of the living and the dead. [43] All the prophets testify about him that everyone who believes in him receives forgiveness of sins through his name."

[44] While Peter was still speaking these words, the Holy Spirit came on all who heard the message. [45] The circumcised believers (Jews) *who had come with Peter were astonished that the gift of the Holy Spirit had been poured out **even on Gentiles**. [46] For they heard them speaking in tongues and praising God.*

*Then Peter said, [47] "Surely no one can stand in the way of their being baptized with water. **They have received the Holy Spirit just as we have.**" [48] So he ordered that they be baptized in the name of Jesus Christ. Then they asked Peter to stay with them for a few days.* (Acts 10:7-48).

Heirs According to the Promise

On the day of Pentecost, those who were added to the church were Jews. With the obedience of Cornelius and his household, (Gentiles), the promise of God to Abraham that through his seed (Christ) all nations of the earth would be blessed was guaranteed.

[6] So also Abraham "believed God, and it was credited to him as righteousness." [7] Understand, then, that those who have faith are children of Abraham. [8] Scripture foresaw that God would justify the Gentiles by faith, and announced the gospel in advance to Abraham: "All nations will be blessed through you." [9] So those who rely on faith are blessed along with Abraham, the man of faith --

[14] He redeemed us in order that the blessing given to Abraham might come to the Gentiles through Christ Jesus, so that by faith we might receive the promise of the Spirit --

48

¹⁶ The promises were spoken to Abraham and to his seed. Scripture does not say "and to seeds," meaning many people, but "and to your seed," meaning one person, who is Christ --

²⁶ So in Christ Jesus you are all children of God through faith, ²⁷ for all of you who were baptized into Christ have clothed yourselves with Christ. ²⁸ There is neither Jew nor Gentile, neither slave nor free, nor is there male and female, for you are all one in Christ Jesus. ²⁹ If you belong to Christ, then you are Abraham's seed, and heirs according to the promise. (Galatians 3:6-9; 14-16; 26-29).

That means that you and I, because of our faith in Jesus Christ, regardless of race, color, gender, or station in life, are heirs according to the promise and part of the kingdom of God!

6

THE CHURCH ON EARTH AS IT IS IN HEAVEN[16]

Apprehension of Death is Normal

It has been said that growing old isn't too bad when you consider the alternative. That may or may not be an accurate statement, depending on the condition of our spiritual lives. It is a fact that when we are born, we begin to die, physically. James, the brother of Jesus, said, *"…What is your life? You are a mist that appears for a little while and then vanishes."* (James 4:14b).

When we are children, time seems to pass very slowly from one birthday to the next; but as we mature, we see time slipping right through our fingers. And the older we get, we finally begin to understand the brevity of our stay on this earth. We begin to realize that someday soon, death may even knock on our door.

I suppose it's natural for everyone to experience some apprehension when contemplating the unknown. But the faithful child of God has no need to fear the end of physical life, because we will continue to live spiritually with Christ. Jesus said, *"[21] To the one who is victorious, I will give the right to sit with me on my throne,"* (Revelation 3:21).

Yes, apprehension is quite normal, but be comforted that the Bible gives us a glimmer of what to expect. No, we don't know exactly what it will be like, but we can be sure that it will be amazing!

Jesus WILL Come Again

After his resurrection, Jesus appeared to the eleven remaining apostles as they went to Galilee, to the mountain where Jesus had told them to go. There he gave them what we have called the great commission.

*[18] Then Jesus came to them and said, "All authority in heaven and on earth has been given to me. [19] **Therefore go and make disciples of all nations, baptizing them** in the name of the Father and of the Son and of the Holy Spirit, [20] and **teaching them to obey everything I have commanded you.** And surely I am with you always, to the **very end of the age.**"* (Matthew 28:18-20).

GO -- MAKE DISCIPLES OF ALL NATIONS -- BAPTIZE THEM -- TEACH THEM. That recipe is good until the end of the age.

[1] "Do not let your hearts be troubled. You believe in God; believe also in me. [2] My Father's house has many rooms; if that were not so, would I have told you that I am going there to prepare a place for you? [3] And if I go and prepare a place for you, I will come back and take you to be with me that you also may be where I am. [4] You know the way to the place where I am going." [5] Thomas said to him, "Lord, we don't know where you are going, so how can we know the way?"

[6] Jesus answered, "I am the way and the truth and the life. No one comes to the Father except through me. [7] If you really know me, you will know my Father as well. From now on, you do know him and have seen him." (John 14:1-7).

Jesus said to his disciples: *[7] "It is not for you to know the times or dates the Father has set by his own authority. [8] But you will receive power when the Holy Spirit comes on you; and you will be my witnesses in Jerusalem, and in all Judea and Samaria, and to the ends of the earth." [9] After he said this, he was taken up before their very eyes, and a cloud hid him from* *their sight. ¹⁰ They were looking intently up into the sky as he was going, when suddenly two men dressed in white stood beside them. ¹¹ "Men of Galilee," they said, "why do you stand here looking into the sky? **This same Jesus, who has been taken from you into heaven, will come back in the same way you have seen him go into heaven.**"* (Acts 1:7-11).

²⁰ He who testifies to these things says, "Yes, I am coming soon." (Revelation 22:20).

He Will Come Unexpectedly*¹⁷*

³⁶ But about that day or hour no one knows, not even the angels in heaven, nor the Son, but only the Father. ³⁷ As it was in the days of Noah, so it will be at the coming of the Son of Man. ³⁸ For in the days before the flood, people were eating and drinking, marrying and giving in marriage, up to the day Noah entered the ark; ³⁹ and they knew nothing about what would happen until the flood came and took them all away. That is how it will be at the coming of the Son of Man. (Matthew 24:36-39).

³² "But about that day or hour no one knows, not even the angels in heaven, nor the Son, but only the Father. *³³ Be on guard! Be alert! You do not know when that time will come. ³⁴ It's like a man going away: He leaves his house and puts his servants in charge, each with their assigned task, and tells the one at the door to keep watch. ³⁵ "Therefore keep watch because you do not know when the owner of the house will come back— whether in the evening, or at midnight, or when the rooster crows, or at dawn. ³⁶ If he comes suddenly, do not let him find you sleeping. ³⁷ What I say to you, I say to everyone: 'Watch!'"* (Mark 13:32-37).

"¹⁰ But the day of the Lord will come like a thief." (2 Peter 3:10a).

His Coming Will Be Visible and Audible

25 "There will be signs in the sun, moon and stars. On the earth, nations will be in anguish and perplexity at the roaring and tossing of the sea. 26 People will faint from terror, apprehensive of what is coming on the world, for the heavenly bodies will be shaken. 27 At that time they will see the Son of Man coming in a cloud with power and great glory. 28 When these things begin to take place, stand up and lift up your heads, because your redemption is drawing near." (Luke 21:25-28).

16 For the Lord himself will come down from heaven, with a loud command, with the voice of the archangel and with the trumpet call of God, and the dead in Christ will rise first. 17 After that, we who are still alive and are left will be caught up together with them in the clouds to meet the Lord in the air. And so we will be with the lord forever. 18Therefore encourage one another with these words." (1 Thessalonians 4:16-18).

"Look, he is coming with the clouds," and "every eye will see him, even those who pierced him;" and all peoples on earth will mourn because of him." So shall it be! Amen. (Revelation 1:7).

He Will Be with a Host of Angels

31 "When the Son of Man comes in his glory, and all the angels with him, he will sit on his glorious throne." (Matthew 25:31).

He Will Bring with Him the Spirits of His Saints

13 Brothers and sisters, we do not want you to be uninformed about those who sleep in death, so that you do not grieve like the rest of mankind, who have no hope. 14 For we believe that Jesus died and rose again, and so we believe that God will bring with Jesus those who have fallen asleep in him." (1 Thessalonians 4:13-14).

54

"¹⁴ Enoch, the seventh from Adam, prophesied about them: "See, the Lord is coming with thousands upon thousands of his holy ones." (Jude v.14).

There will be Resurrection from the Dead

"At that time Michael, the great prince who protects your people, will arise. There will be a time of distress such as has not happened from the beginning of nations until then. But at that time your people—everyone whose name is found written in the book—will be delivered. ²Multitudes who sleep in the dust of the earth will awake: some to everlasting life, others to shame and everlasting contempt. ³Those who are wise will shine like the brightness of the heavens, and those who lead many to righteousness, like the stars for ever and ever." Daniel 12:1-3).

The Dead in Christ will Rise First

Christ was first to be resurrected with his glorified body! Next, when Christ returns, all those who belong to Christ will be resurrected with their glorified, imperishable bodies!

²⁰ But Christ has indeed been raised from the dead, the firstfruits of those who have fallen asleep. ²¹ For since death came through a man, the resurrection of the dead comes also through a man. ²² For as in Adam all die, so in Christ all will be made alive. ²³ But each in turn: Christ, the firstfruits; then, when he comes, those who belong to him. (1 Corinthians 15:20-23).

¹⁵ "According to the Lord's word, we tell you that we who are still alive, who are left until the coming of the Lord, will certainly not precede those who have fallen asleep. ¹⁶ For the Lord himself will come down from heaven, with a loud command, with the voice of the archangel and with the trumpet call of God, and the dead in Christ will rise first." (1 Thessalonians 4:15-16).

The Living will be Changed

17 After that, we who are still alive and are left will be caught up together with them in the clouds to meet the Lord in the air. And so we will be with the Lord forever. (1 Thessalonians 4:17).

51 Listen, I tell you a mystery: We will not all sleep, but we will all be changed— 52 in a flash, in the twinkling of an eye, at the last trumpet. For the trumpet will sound, the dead will be raised imperishable, and we will be changed. 53 For the perishable must clothe itself with the imperishable, and the mortal with immortality. 54 When the perishable has been clothed with the imperishable, and the mortal with immortality, then the saying that is written will come true: "Death has been swallowed up in victory." (1 Corinthians 15:51-54).

Christ will be our Judge

22 "Moreover, the Father judges no one, but has entrusted all judgment to the Son, 23 that all may honor the Son just as they honor the Father. Whoever does not honor the Son does not honor the Father, who sent him." (John 5:22, 27).

30 In the past God overlooked such ignorance, but now he commands all people everywhere to repent. 31 For he has set a day when he will judge the world with justice by the man he has appointed. He has given proof of this to everyone by raising him from the dead." (Acts 17:31).

"For none of us lives for ourselves alone, and none of us dies for ourselves alone. 8 If we live, we live for the Lord; and if we die, we die for the Lord. So, whether we live or die, we belong to the Lord. 9 For this very reason, Christ died and returned to life so that he might be the Lord of both the dead and the living. 10 You, then, why do you judge your brother

or sister? Or why do you treat them with contempt? For we will all stand before God's judgment seat. (Romans 14:7-11).

[10] For we must all appear before the judgment seat of Christ, so that each of us may receive what is due us for the things done while in the body, whether good or bad." (2 Corinthians 5:10).

He will Divide the "Sheep" (Righteous) from the "Goats" (Unrighteous)

[31] "When the Son of Man comes in his glory, and all the angels with him, he will sit on his glorious throne. [32] All the nations will be gathered before him, and he will separate the people one from another as a shepherd separates the sheep from the goats. [33] He will put the sheep on his right and the goats on his left. [34]Then the King will say to those on his right, 'Come, you who are blessed by my Father; take your inheritance, the kingdom prepared for you since the creation of the world.'" [41] Then he will say to those on his left, 'Depart from me, you who are cursed, into the eternal fire prepared for the devil and his angels." (Matthew 25:32-34, 41).

The Righteous will be Rewarded

[7] "No, we declare God's wisdom, a mystery that has been hidden and that God destined for our glory before time began. [8] None of the rulers of this age understood it, for if they had, they would not have crucified the Lord of glory.[9]

However, as it is written:

"What no eye has seen,
what no ear has heard,

and what no human mind has conceived—
the things God has prepared for those who love him."

Hebrews 11:16 - *[13] "All these people were still living by faith when they died. They did not receive the things promised; they only saw them and welcomed them from a distance, admitting that they were foreigners and strangers on earth. [14] People who say such things show that they are looking for a country of their own. [15] If they had been thinking of the country they had left, they would have had opportunity to return. [16] Instead, they were longing for a better country—a heavenly one. Therefore God is not ashamed to be called their God, for he has prepared a city for them."* (1 Corinthians 2:7-9).

[3] "Praise be to the God and Father of our Lord Jesus Christ! In his great mercy he has given us new birth into a living hope through the resurrection of Jesus Christ from the dead, [4] and into an inheritance that can never perish, spoil or fade. This inheritance is kept in heaven for you, [5] who through faith are shielded by God's power until the coming of the salvation that is ready to be revealed in the last time." (1 Peter 1:3, 4).

The Kingdom on the Earth Will be Delivered Up to God; Christ Will Put Down All Rule and Authority *[18]*

[24] "Then the end will come, when he hands over the kingdom to God the Father after he has destroyed all dominion, authority and power. [25] For he must reign until he has put all his enemies under his feet. [26] The last enemy to be destroyed is death. [27] For he "has put everything under his feet." Now when it says that "everything" has been put under him, it is clear that this does not include God himself, who put everything under Christ. [28] When he has done this, then the Son himself will be made subject to him who put everything under him, so that God may be all in all." (1 Corinthians 15:24-28).

58

The church in Corinth wanted to know about the resurrection and how the dead will be raised. Paul explained:

35 But someone will ask, "How are the dead raised? With what kind of body will they come?" 36 How foolish! What you sow does not come to life unless it dies. 37 When you sow, you do not plant the body that will be, but just a seed, perhaps of wheat or of something else. 38 But God gives it a body as he has determined, and to each kind of seed he gives its own body. 39 Not all flesh is the same: People have one kind of flesh, animals have another, birds another and fish another. 40 There are also heavenly bodies and there are earthly bodies; but the splendor of the heavenly bodies is one kind, and the splendor of the earthly bodies is another. 41 The sun has one kind of splendor, the moon another and the stars another; and star differs from star in splendor.42 So will it be with the resurrection of the dead. The body that is sown is perishable, it is raised imperishable; 43 it is sown in dishonor, it is raised in glory; it is sown in weakness, it is raised in power; 44 it is sown a natural body, it is raised a spiritual body. If there is a natural body, there is also a spiritual body. (1 Corinthians 15:35-44).

It Will be the Last Day

44 Then Jesus cried out, "Whoever believes in me does not believe in me only, but in the one who sent me. 45 The one who looks at me is seeing the one who sent me. 46 I have come into the world as a light, so that no one who believes in me should stay in darkness. 47 "If anyone hears my words but does not keep them, I do not judge that person. For I did not come to judge the world, but to save the world. 48 There is a judge for the one who rejects me and does not accept my words; the very words I have spoken will condemn them at the last day. 49 For I did not speak on my own, but the Father who sent me commanded me to say all that I have spoken. 50I know that his command leads to eternal life. So whatever I say is just what the Father has told me to say." (John 12:40-54).

" -- but in these last days he has spoken to us by his Son, whom he appointed heir of all things, and through whom also he made the universe." (Hebrews 11:2).

The Bible says that Christ will return with a host of angels and those redeemed who died long ago will be with Christ when he returns.

If I read it correctly, when we die, our souls return to God for whatever joys he has prepared for us until the second coming of Christ on the last day, and the resurrection of our new, glorified, imperishable bodies. The still-living righteous bodies will be changed in the twinkling of an eye to their imperishable bodies and all will join Christ, the angels and the rest of the redeemed in the air. (1 Corinthians 15:51-54; 1 Thessalonians 4:13-17; Jude v.14).

It will be the day of judgment and the old heavens will disappear and old earth will be laid bare.

*[10] But the day of the Lord will come like a thief. The heavens will disappear with a roar; the elements will be destroyed by fire, and the earth and everything done in it will be laid bare. [11] Since everything will be destroyed in this way, what kind of people ought you to be? You ought to live holy and godly lives [12] as you look forward to the day of God and speed its coming. That day will bring about the destruction of the heavens by fire, and the elements will melt in the heat. [13] But in keeping with his promise **we are looking forward to a new heaven and a new earth**, where righteousness dwells. [14] So then, dear friends, since you are looking forward to this, make every effort to be found spotless, blameless and at peace with him.* (2 Peter 3:10-14).

A God of Love and Forgiveness Will Not Punish the Unrighteous, Will He?

For the traditional Christian, heaven is the everlasting dwelling place of God and the angelic beings who have served him faithfully since the beginning. There, those Christians who have been redeemed through faith in Jesus as the Christ will be with him forever in glory.

Protestant Christianity does not offer its followers the opportunities for afterlife redemption afforded by purgatory or any other intermediate spiritual state, but it has removed much of the fear of hell and replaced it with an emphasis upon grace and faith.

While fundamentalist Protestants retain the traditional views of heaven and hell, there are many contemporary Protestant clergy who have rejected the idea of a place of eternal torment for condemned souls as incompatible with the belief in a loving God of forgiveness. Hell has been transformed from a place of everlasting suffering to an afterlife state of being without the presence of God. For liberal Christian theologians, the entire teaching of a place of everlasting damnation has been completely rejected in favor of the love of Jesus for all humanity.

While writing this book, I have tried to maximize the beauties of heaven and not use scare tactics to emphasize the condemnation for the unrighteous. I want you, dear reader, to get a small glimpse of our exciting, eternal future life with our Lord. But for your soul's sake, I must give you encouragement to believe that Jesus Christ is the son of God and the savior of all nations. If I am wrong, and there is no punishment for the unrighteous, I have lost nothing; but if I am right, and you have never confessed him as Lord and Christ, you could be in danger of losing everything.

Many say that Jesus was a good man, but not the Messiah. Let me remind you that if he is not who he said he was, he lied and was not a good man at all.

Those who do not believe that Christ died for our sins should take the Bible seriously, anticipating the Lord's impending return, when every knee will bow, and every mouth will confess that Jesus Christ is Lord. If we don't bow before him in this life, we most certainly will bow before him in the next.

"Therefore God exalted him to the highest place and gave him the name that is above every name, [10]that at the name of Jesus every knee should bow, in heaven and on earth and under the earth, [11] and every tongue acknowledge that Jesus Christ is Lord, to the glory of God the Father." (Philippians 2:9-11).

While God's love is as boundless as His power and knowledge, He is also a just God, and being so requires Him to fulfill His promises. He has promised unspeakable punishment to those who are ungodly and disobedient. Vengeance is also God's. That being the case, and since God does not lie (Titus 1:2), his promise to repay those who turn their backs on his Son will not be denied.

[19] Do not take revenge, my dear friends, but leave room for God's wrath, for it is written: "It is mine to avenge; I will repay," says the Lord. (Romans 12:19).

The Wicked will be Punished

[41] "Then he will say to those on his left, 'Depart from me, you who are cursed, into the eternal fire prepared for the devil and his angels.'" (Matthew 25:41).

[6] "God is just: He will pay back trouble to those who trouble you [7] and give relief to you who are troubled, and to us as well. This will happen when the Lord Jesus is revealed from heaven in blazing fire with his powerful angels. [8] He will punish those who do not know God and do not obey the gospel of our Lord Jesus. [9] They will be punished with everlasting destruction and shut out from the presence of the Lord and from the glory of his might." (2 Thessalonians 1:7-9).

A New Heaven and a New Earth have been Prepared

21 Then I saw "a new heaven and a new earth," for the first heaven and the first earth had passed away, and there was no longer any sea.² I saw the Holy City, the new Jerusalem, coming down out of heaven from God, prepared as a bride beautifully dressed for her husband. ³ And I heard a loud voice from the throne saying, "Look! **God's dwelling place is now among the people, and he will dwell with them.** *They will be his people, and God himself will be with them and be their God...⁵ He who was seated on the throne said, "I am making everything new...⁶ He said to me: "***It is done. I am the Alpha and the Omega, the Beginning and the End.*** *To the thirsty I will give water without cost from the spring of the water of life. ⁷ Those who are victorious will inherit all this, and I will be their God and they will be my children.* (Revelation 21:1-3, 5-7).

The reference of "It is done," is to the work accomplished throughout the whole drama of human history before this eternal state. This statement does not mean that there will be no future works of God, but that a major work has been brought to completion, and that the works now relating to the eternal state are beginning.

7

I'M THERE ALREADY BUT NOT QUITE YET

This World Is Not My Home

This world is not my home I'm just a-passin' through;
My treasures are laid up somewhere beyond the blue;
The angels beckon me from heaven's open door,
And I can't feel at home in this world anymore

Oh Lord, You know I have no friend like you;
If heaven's not my home then Lord what will I do?
The angels beckon me from heaven's open door,
And I can't feel at home in this world anymore.

I have a loving mother just over in glory land;
And I don't expect to stop until I shake her hand;
She's waiting now for me in heaven's open door,
And I can't feel at home in this world anymore.

Oh Lord, You know I have no friend like you;
If heaven's not my home then Lord what will I do?
The angels beckon me from heaven's open door,
And I can't feel at home in this world anymore.

Just over in glory land we'll live eternally;
The saints on every hand are shouting victory;
Their songs of sweetest praise
Drift back from heaven's shore,
And I can't feel at home in this world anymore.

Oh Lord, You know I have no friend like you;
If heaven's not my home then Lord what will I do?
The angels beckon me from heaven's open door,
And I can't feel at home in this world anymore.

In 1962, Jim Reeves recorded this song and it became one of gospel singers' favorite hymns. There are many different opinions about the author of this song, but most attribute it to Alfred Edward Brumley (1905-1977), a popular songwriter from Arkansas. He was a member of a gospel quartet and it is believed that he wrote this song in 1936. As well as teaching singing schools, he wrote more than 800 songs, and was a gospel music editor for decades, working in the publishing business with his five sons. Likely his most popular creation was *I'll Fly Away*.

This song reminds me of the great faith chapter in the Bible, Hebrews 11. After giving many examples of faith from Old Testament characters, the writer says in verses 13-16,

[13] These all died in faith, not having received the promises, but seeing them afar off and believing them and embracing them and confessing that they were strangers and pilgrims on the earth. [14] For those that say such things declare plainly that they seek their native country. [15] And truly, if they had been mindful of that country from which they came out, they might have had time to have returned. [16] But now they desire a better country, that is, a heavenly one; therefore, God is not ashamed to be called their God, for he has prepared for them a city.

In the World, But Not of the World [19]

When we read of the "world" in the New Testament, we are reading the Greek word *cosmos*. *Cosmos* most often refers to the inhabited earth and the people who live on the earth, which functions apart from God. Satan is the ruler of this "cosmos," (John 12:31; 16:11; 1 John 5:19). By the simple definition that the word *world* refers to a world system ruled by Satan, we can more readily appreciate Christ's claims that believers are no longer of the world—we are no longer ruled by sin, nor are we bound by the principles of the world.

In addition, we are being changed into the image of Christ, causing our interest in the things of the world to become less and less as we mature in Christ.

Believers in Jesus Christ are simply in the world—physically present—but not of it, not originating from it, not part of its values. (John 17:14-15). As believers, we should be set apart from the world. This is the meaning of being holy and living a holy, righteous life—to be set apart. We are not to engage in the sinful activities the world promotes, nor are we to retain the insipid, corrupt mind that the world creates. Rather, we are to conform ourselves, and our minds, to that of Jesus Christ (Romans 12:1-2). This is a daily activity and commitment.

The Church in Heavenly Realms, NOW

The task of the church is to make the kingdom visible. We do that by living in such a way that we bear witness to the reality of the kingship of Christ in our jobs, our families, our schools, and even our checkbooks, because God in Christ is King over every one of these spheres of life. The only way the kingdom of God is going to be manifest in this world before Christ comes is if we manifest it by the way we live as citizens of heaven and subjects of the King.

The church exists primarily for two closely correlated purposes: to worship God and to work for his kingdom in the world -- The church also exists for a third purpose, which serves the other two: to encourage one another, to build one another up in faith, to pray with and for one another,

67

to learn from one another and teach one another, and to set one another examples to follow, challenges to take up, and urgent tasks to perform. This is all part of what is known loosely as fellowship.[20]

While we are on earth, we are doing life the best we can, trying to be righteous and failing miserably. Like Paul and every other person who has ever lived, we do things we don't want to do, and we don't do things we know we should do, *but thanks be to God, who delivers* (us) *through Jesus Christ our Lord!* (Romans 7:21-25, parentheses mine, SM).

So we wait -- until we die or until Christ returns to gather us to himself. Because of Christ, we will be in the new creation to participate in everything high and holy. But while we are waiting, we must also understand that being in the world, but not of it, is necessary if we are to be a light to those who are in spiritual darkness. We are to live in such a way that those outside the faith can see our good deeds and our manner and know that there is something "different" about us. As Christians, we should be examples to those around us and exhibit the fruit of the Spirit within us.

Listen to this quote from Charles Spurgeon:

> *"See the happiness which is promised us! Behold the heaven which awaits us! Forget for awhile your present cares: let all your difficulties and your sorrows vanish for a season; and live for awhile in the future which is so certified by faithful promises that you may rejoice in it even now! The veil which parts us from our great reward is very thin: hope gazes through its gauzy fabric. Faith, with eagle eyes, penetrates the mist which hides eternal delights from longing eyes."* [21]

The apostle Paul, wrote to the church in Ephesus, *³ Praise be to the God and Father of our Lord Jesus Christ, who has blessed us in the **heavenly realms** with every spiritual blessing in Christ.⁴ For he chose us in him before the creation of the world to be holy and blameless in his sight. In* *love ⁵ he pre-destined us for adoption to sonship through Jesus Christ, in accordance with his pleasure and will — ⁶ to the praise of his glorious grace, which he has freely given us in the One he loves. ⁷ In him we have redemption through his blood, the forgiveness of sins, in accordance with the riches of God's grace ⁸ that he lavished on us. With all wisdom and under-standing, ⁹ he made known to us the mystery of his will according to his good pleasure, which he purposed in Christ, ¹⁰ to be put into effect when the times reach their fulfillment — to bring unity to all things in heaven and on earth under Christ.* (Ephesians 1:4-10).

Where is Home for You?

My father was born in Childersburg, Alabama. My mother was born in Rockmart, Georgia. What are the odds for that man and that woman to meet, get married, and give birth to a daughter in Gadsden, Alabama, who would end up in Roswell, Georgia? Roswell is my home -- on earth. But my REAL home is the one that Jesus Christ went to prepare for me.

Sometimes we ask strangers, where do you live? It helps us to know them a little better. So what does *home* mean to you? I think we will all agree that it is not merely a house, or city, or country. It's a feeling. And that feeling is a major force, *love*. Home is where we gather our loved ones around us; where we can love and be loved.

For many reasons we may go away from home for a while; we may be on vacation or visiting friends, or for more difficult reasons of a hospital stay due to illness, or travel because of the death of a loved one; or painful separation from our loved ones because of one being sentenced to prison, or evacuation of our home because of natural disasters such as fire or flooding. Even when leaving home is pleasant, it is often said that we are glad to be home again.

A Home Prepared for Us

Our Lord Jesus told his disciples during his earthly ministry that he did not have a place to lay his head. (Matthew 8:20). And Paul described some of those who were in service for Christ as being homeless. (1

Corinthians 4:11). Yet, Jesus promised that he was going to prepare a home for them (including us).

*"Do not let your hearts be troubled. You believe in God; believe also in me. ² My Father's house has many rooms; if that were not so, would I have told you that I am going there to prepare a place for you? ³ And if I go and prepare a place for you, **I will come back** and take you to be with me that you also may be where I am."* (John 14:1-3).

Before his death, Jesus comforted his disciples with the promise that he would go to provide a place for them. The most beautiful part was his assurance that he would return for them and receive them unto himself.

Considering mansions by the world's standards, I know they don't in any way come close to the mansions prepared for the saints in heaven. No matter how spectacular the mansions in our Father's house, dwelling with Jesus will be the most beautiful habitation of all. Welcomed into heaven by the Way, the Truth, and the Life will be the culmination of the hope we have in Christ.

The church is the spiritual kingdom of God on earth NOW. **But the kingdom of God in heaven has never been about NOW.** It has always been about being prepared for a time to come. The prophet Isaiah spoke of the coming of the new heaven and new earth. Jesus taught his disciples to be prepared for his return. John the apostle saw the Revelation of Jesus Christ on the isle of Patmos — the beauty of the new heaven and new earth — revealing those things that had been hidden in prophecies before.

Believers understand that this earth is not our home. We were created for the new heaven and new earth that God has prepared for us. We cannot say exactly what that will be like because we have yet to experience it. But I don't think it will be like we are in church forever and ever. I believe the Bible indicates that our imperishable bodies will be standing on the solid ground of the new earth, that we will have work to do, food to enjoy, and people we know and love, including children, babies, and animals! I believe there will be music and singing — even God's singing!

(Zephaniah 3:17). I believe there will be exquisite, colorful flowers, delicious fruit, and many other wonders of nature to enjoy — all without the interference of Satan!

We cannot imagine such beauty! We hope to see the face of God and worship him; we hope to walk with Jesus, and that the Holy Spirit will supply our every need. We know that it will be an eternally perfect existence without sin and sorrow, and we will again have access to the tree of life!

I believe that the new heaven and new earth will be a place of endless joy and love. Believers must know that this is our great hope to live righteously on earth. It is our preparation for an eternal destiny of infinite fascination and excitement. In fact, because of our complete faith and hope in what is to come, we live with anticipation as if we were already there.

Awaiting the New Body

Paul states that he is confident in his eternal destiny and longs for the day when he can be "absent from the body" and be present with the Lord he loves and serves. To be "absent" from one's body simply means to die, because at death, the spirit is separated from the body and moves into its eternal abode. Christians are always confident, knowing that while we are at home in the body, we are absent from the presence of God. For we walk by faith, not by sight. We are confident that to be absent from the body and to be present with the Lord is far better for us.

Further, Paul says, *For we know that if the earthly tent we live in is destroyed, we have a building from God, an eternal house in heaven, not built by human hands. [2] Meanwhile we groan, longing to be clothed instead with our heavenly dwelling, [3] because when we are clothed, we will not be found naked. [4] For while we are in this tent, we groan and are burdened, because we do not wish to be unclothed but to be clothed instead with our heavenly dwelling, so that what is mortal may be swallowed up by life. [5] Now the one who has fashioned us for this very purpose is God, who has given us the Spirit as a deposit, guaranteeing what is to come.*

⁶ Therefore we are always confident and know that as long as we are at home in the body we are away from the Lord. ⁷ For we live by faith, not by sight. ⁸ We are confident, I say, and would prefer to be away from the body and at home with the Lord. ⁹ So we make it our goal to please him, whether we are at home in the body or away from it. ¹⁰ For we must all appear before the judgment seat of Christ, so that each of us may receive what is due us for the things done while in the body, whether good or bad. (2 Corinthians 5:1-10).

Not from a Worldly Point of View

¹⁴ For Christ's love compels us, because we are convinced that one died for all, and therefore all died. ¹⁵ And he died for all, that those who live should no longer live for themselves but for him who died for them and was raised again. ¹⁶ So from now on we regard no one from a worldly point of view. Though we once regarded Christ in this way, we do so no longer. ¹⁷ Therefore, if anyone is in Christ, the new creation has come: The old has gone, the new is here! (2 Corinthians 5:14-21).

Again, to the Galatians, Paul said, *¹⁴ May I never boast except in the cross of our Lord Jesus Christ, through which the world has been crucified to me, and I to the world. ¹⁵ Neither circumcision* (Jew) *nor uncircumcision* (Gentile) *means anything; what counts is the new creation.* (Galatians 6:14-15, parentheses mine, SM).

God's Vision is Greater Than Ours

Did you ever take your hand or your finger and cover up an object you see in the distance? Like putting your hand over the moon or your finger over a star? You know that the objects are a lot bigger than they appear. You can imagine that you can erase a star from the sky with one touch of your finger tip, but you know that's not true. You see, God sees things for what they really are, and we only see them from our finite existence.

What God sees for your life is so much bigger and better than what you can see right now. And what he has planned for those who love him is so indescribable that we cannot even imagine it!

We know that the earth we live in is big! It takes days to drive from Florida to California and it takes days in a jumbo jet to get from the United States to the other side of the world. But the earth is microscopic in size compared to some stars! There is a star named Canis Majoris that is 1 billion times the size of the sun. Canis Majoris is a hypergiant star located 3,900 light years from Earth. Over 3.7 quadrillion earths could fit into the star Canis Majoris! Yet we might be able to cover it up with the tip of our finger.

We serve a big God who is calling us into bigger things. Let's not settle for the "here-and-now, this-is-all-there-is" mentality.

[9] However, as it is written:

"What no eye has seen,
what no ear has heard,
and what no human mind has conceived" —
the things God has prepared for those who love him—
(1 Corinthians 2:9).

8

A SHORT STUDY OF THE BOOK
OF REVELATION

A Difficult Read Made Somewhat Simple

I AM A SIMPLE-MINDED PERSON. BY THAT I MEAN THAT I
am not a degreed theological genius in any sense of the word. But I love
the Bible; it fascinates me. It contains many subjects that are hard to
understand, and they are, but I accept the challenge of learning as much
as I can about them, then translating them into easy-to-understand language that may help others to understand. But don't take my word for it,
you should study for yourselves.

Revelation is the last book in our New Testament. I became intrigued
with it in the 1980's and have read it and read about it many times over
the years. I sincerely appreciate those Bible scholars who have helped
me to understand a little more now than I did then. However, it is a book
shrouded in mystery. Many people think that Revelation cannot be understood; that the book is intended to be hard. But judge for yourselves.

Please enter this study with an open mind. Try to erase any precon-
ceived notions you may have. Study the book of Revelation for yourself.
I believe this is one of the primary reasons that people have difficulty
with the book. Many do not read and study the book of Revelation for
themselves. Instead, they just listen to what everyone else has to say

about the book. This leads to great confusion because everyone may say something different about the book. You must read the book for yourself. You need to rely on God's word and your own study of the book, rather than relying on my study.

John's book is a prophetic work which concerns the imminent and inaugurated fulfillment of Old Testament prophecies about the kingdom in Jesus Christ. There is a war raging in the lives of God's children. I read the last chapter -- **we win!!**

Greetings and Doxology

¹ The revelation from Jesus Christ, which God gave him to show his servants what must soon take place. He made it known by sending his angel to his servant John, ² who testifies to everything he saw—that is, the word of God and the testimony of Jesus Christ. ³ Blessed is the one who reads aloud the words of this prophecy and blessed are those who hear it and take to heart what is written in it, because the time is near.

⁴ John, To the seven churches in the province of Asia:

Grace and peace to you from him who is, and who was, and who is to come, and from the seven spirits before his throne, ⁵ and from Jesus Christ, who is the faithful witness, the firstborn from the dead, and the ruler of the kings of the earth. To him who loves us and has freed us from our sins by his blood, ⁶ and has made us to be a kingdom and priests to serve his God and Father—to him be glory and power for ever and ever! Amen.

"Look, he is coming with the clouds,"
and "every eye will see him,
even those who pierced him";
and all peoples on earth "will mourn because of him." So shall it be! Amen. (Revelation 1:1-8).

The Revelation of Jesus Christ

"'Revelation' means to expose in full view what was formerly hidden, veiled, or secret" [22] This is a significant beginning to our study. The book of Revelation is revealing something that previously was concealed. Revelation is not code. Revelation is not hidden language. To suggest such violates the very name of the book.

This is the book of unveiling. This is the book of revealing, not concealing. This information also sets up our filter for our interpretation method. This book is explaining things that were previously hidden. While we do not know for certain yet, our most likely source would be Old Testament prophecies that were shrouded in mystery that the book is going to make plain. It is noted by most scholars that Revelation borrows heavily from the images of the Old Testament. Therefore, our interpretative model should be that the book of Revelation is an explanation of those Old Testament images. When we read language in Revelation that is found in the Old Testament, we need to go back to the origin of the image and understand it in its proper context. Then we can see how the book of Revelation is shedding light or revealing information about that prophecy. It is not "revelations," but "revelation." One unveiling of the things hidden in the past.

This is *"the revelation from Jesus Christ, which God gave him to show to his servants...."* God gave this revelation to Jesus who gave it to his servants. The end of the book of Revelation makes the point again that this revelation is from Jesus. *"I, Jesus, have sent my angel to testify to you about these things for the churches."* (Revelation 22:16).

Time-Markers

There are two time-markers in this preface. The first is found in verse 1, *"To show his servants the things that must soon take place."* The second time-marker is in verse 3, *"For the time is near."* Carefully read those time-markers. Verse 1 says that the revelation concerns things that must soon take place. The time is near for the events that are contained in the revelation and that is why those who read, hear, and keep the words are blessed. The point cannot be ignored. The things in the book are happening soon. Because of these time-markers, scholars are beginning to rightly reject the popular futurist view that the book of Revelation has not occurred yet.

Remember that God is not bound by time in the same way that people are. However, God is bound by time when he speaks to humans and reveals to them that something *"must soon take place"* and *"the time is near."* God is not bound by time, but he is bound by his word when he speaks to humanity. If he tells humans that something must happen soon and the time is near, then it must be soon to us and near to us.

One of the themes of Revelation is relief from suffering will come soon. Hundreds or thousands of years will not work. The book of Revelation is not a book about current events. We must not read the newspapers and try to plug what is happening today as the fulfillment of the book of Revelation. The book of Revelation was relevant to the first century Christians who heard its message.

Notice in verse 3 that those Christians in the first century who read, heard, and kept what is written in it would be blessed. If chapters 4-22 are yet to come still, then there is no blessing for those Christians who received this letter. This does not mean that there is nothing for us to learn. We learn from every book in the Bible even though there was an original audience to whom the book was written. We do not read Romans and discard its value because it was written to the Christians in the city of Rome in the first century. There is still great value, lessons, and applications for us. The book of Revelation is the same. Though written to the seven churches of Asia, there is still great value, lessons, and applications for us.

When we communicate with one another, we assume that we are speaking literally, unless something in our language demands us to take it symbolically. We study the scriptures the same way. We take the words of God literally and straightforward unless something in the text demands an idiomatic or figurative interpretation.

When Jesus started talking about planks and logs in our eyes, we know that Jesus is speaking figuratively, using imagery to teach a principle. With the book of Revelation, the preface has told us to reverse our method. The book has been put into symbols and signs. Therefore, we should read the book as symbols unless something in the text demands otherwise.

Now, let me make an important point. Just because Revelation is full of symbols does not mean that there is not a literal or historical fulfillment. The images can represent a literal or historical event. The book of Revelation is not fanciful myths and stories. The symbol can represent something actual and real. The red, octagonal stop sign represents the literal act of stopping one's car. The point is that we should read Revelation seeking the meaning behind the images. We cannot take the numbers, locusts, scorpions, dragons, beasts and other images found in the book at face value. They represent something and our goal as readers is to determine the meaning of those symbols. We take the book as symbols representing something unless something clearly shows us that the image is not symbolic.

We need to observe one other point. While the book of Revelation is a letter to the seven churches of Asia, we must also recognize that it is prophetic in nature. Verse 3 of chapter 1 describes this book as, *"The words of this prophecy."* This book communicates the inspired messages of God and it is showing its first century audience the things that are about to come soon. This is important for us as we try to interpret Revelation's symbols into a historical context. The things that the book reveals do not have to be happening at the moment the book is written. The book is speaking of things about to happen soon.

How exciting to read the book of Revelation which will unfold and unveil the prophecies concealed in the past! We stand at a fortunate time to look back and see the completion of God's plan and are also blessed when we read, hear, and keep the things written in this prophetic book. The book of Revelation is a message of encouragement and hope during difficult times. Our faith will be bolstered by studying the messages contained in this book. Let us hear the words of this book, read the words of this book, keep what is written in this book, and be blessed in doing so.

In chapter 1:5, John proceeds to give several descriptions of Jesus. He is called the faithful witness, the firstborn of the dead, and the ruler of the kings on earth. These three descriptions are found in Psalm 89. Psalm 89:37 describes the Messianic offspring of David as a faithful witness. In Psalm 89:27 the Messianic offspring of David is described as the firstborn and the highest of the kings of the earth. All three images reveal Jesus as the Davidic king who rules on the throne. As the faithful witness, Jesus' rule will endure forever as the sun (Psalm 89:36-37).

Jesus is the first fruits of the resurrection. His resurrection proves his authority and proves he is ruling from his throne. Ruler of the kings of the earth shows Jesus' absolute power over all rulers, kings, and kingdoms. Revelation refers to Psalm 89 to show the fulfillment of the promises made to David regarding the eternal kingdom. Jesus is on that throne. By quoting Psalm 89 the book of Revelation is setting up the conflict between the exalted Christ and the earthly rulers. Even more to the point, Jesus is still in charge and is still ruling even though there are other rulers who will cause the people of God to suffer.

He will call out to me, 'You are my Father, my God, the Rock my Savior.' [27] And I will appoint him to be my firstborn, the most exalted of the kings of the earth. [28] I will maintain my love to him forever, and my covenant with him will never fail. [29] I will establish his line forever, his throne as long as the heavens endure --

Once for all, I have sworn by my holiness — and I will not lie to David — [36] that his line will continue forever and his throne endure before me like the sun; [37] it will be established forever like the moon, the faithful witness in the sky. (Psalm 89:26-29, 36-37).

The end of verse 5 and all of verse 6 is a statement of praise and glory to Jesus for what he has done. Jesus has loved us. Loving us is the reason that he died. Even during our difficult times and suffering, Jesus still loves us. He has freed us from our sins by his blood. These benefits are derived through his blood, that is, in his death on the cross. If Jesus is the king, which the previous verse asserted, then we are citizens in his kingdom. The readers are not citizens in the Roman Empire, not citizens in Judaism, but are citizens in the kingdom of Christ. Jesus has provided a new family relationship by which all believers have a priestly ministry to God. We are subjects in Christ's kingdom with direct priestly access to God.

Passages like Isaiah 65:17, Isaiah 66:22, and 2 Peter 3:10-13 confirm our understanding of the new heaven and new earth as the time when righteousness rules. This world, with all its evil, pain, and difficulties, has passed away. Now we are at home with the Lord (2 Corinthians 5:8).

"See, I will create new heavens and a new earth. The former things will not be remembered, nor will they come to mind. (Isaiah 65:17).

22 "As the new heavens and the new earth that I make will endure before me," declares the LORD, "so will your name and descendants endure. (Isaiah 66:22).

10 But the day of the Lord will come like a thief. The heavens will disappear with a roar; the elements will be destroyed by fire, and the earth and everything done in it will be laid bare.

11 Since everything will be destroyed in this way, what kind of people ought you to be? You ought to live holy and godly lives 12 as you look forward to the day of God and speed its coming. That day will bring about the destruction of the heavens by fire, and the elements will melt in the heat. 13 But in keeping with his promise we are looking forward to a new heaven and a new earth, where righteousness dwells. (2 Peter 3:10-13).

Revelation 21:9 - John sees one of the seven angels who had poured out one of the bowls of wrath. The angel tells John that he is going show him the bride, the wife of the Lamb. We already know from the scriptures what is going to be described to us. Revelation 19:7-8 told us that the marriage of the Lamb has come, and the bride is ready. The bride is defined for us as the saints, God's holy people, and the fine linen the bride is wearing represents the righteous deeds of the saints. Paul makes the same connection, describing how husbands love their wives as how Christ loves the church. Christ is the husband, the groom and the church, the people of God, are the wife, the bride.

The description the angel gives is not a description of a literal new city to be built in Palestine. The city, new Jerusalem, represents the people of God, the church. Notice the other New Testament authors who make the same connection. The apostle Paul described the Jerusalem that is from above as the children of promise, the people of God (Galatians 4:21-31). The writer of Hebrews spoke the same of the new Jerusalem.

22 But you have come to Mount Zion, to the city of the living God, the heavenly Jerusalem. You have come to thousands upon thousands of angels in joyful assembly, 23 to the church of the firstborn, whose names are written in heaven. You have come to God, the Judge of all, to the spirits of the righteous made perfect, 24 to Jesus the mediator of a new covenant, and to the sprinkled blood that speaks a better word than the blood of Abel. (Hebrews 12:22-24).

The angel carries John away in the Spirit to show him the holy city Jerusalem coming down out of heaven from God. Being carried in the Spirit reminds us that John continues a visionary sequence (Revelation 1:10; 4:2). **John has not been literally carried anywhere. He is seeing a vision from God.** The holy city Jerusalem coming down out of heaven connects back to Revelation 21:2. We saw the new heaven, new earth, and new Jerusalem introduced.

Verses 3-8 gave more details about the new heaven and new earth. The rest of the chapter gives more details about new Jerusalem.

New Jerusalem's Walls and Gates (21:11-14)

John sees the new Jerusalem having the glory of God, full of radiance like a rare jewel, clear as crystal. The picture is likely similar to the gleam and shimmer of a beautiful diamond. The people of God are symbolized as a great city coming down from heaven, shining with the glory of God.

Verses 12-14 describes the walls and the gates of the city. The great, high wall represents how the unclean and wicked cannot enter into fellowship with God. Notice this point is clearly made in verse 27.

"But nothing unclean will ever enter it, nor anyone who does what is detestable or false, but only those who are written in the Lamb's book of life."

The walls show that no one can enter unless they are in fellowship with the Lord. The walls and gates also picture the prophecy that Isaiah made.

In that day this song will be sung in the land of Judah:
We have a strong city;
  God makes salvation
  its walls and ramparts.
² Open the gates
  that the righteous nation may enter,
  the nation that keeps faith. (Isaiah 26:1, 2).

The other prophetic references come from Ezekiel's vision of the new temple in Ezekiel 40-48. In Ezekiel's context the physical temple has been destroyed and the people carried into captivity. Ezekiel, in a vision, is taken to a very high mountain like John was for this vision in Revelation. Ezekiel sees a great new temple. Revelation borrows many images and descriptions from Ezekiel's vision showing the fulfillment of what Ezekiel prophesied. Ezekiel's vision describes the actual presence of God within the temple of the new community.

John sees twelve gates guarded by twelve angels. Inscribed on the gates were the names of the twelve tribes of the sons of Israel. Ezekiel saw the same thing (Ezekiel 48:30-35). There are three gates on each side of the city, each inscribed with a name from sons of Israel. In addition to the twelve gates, there are twelve foundation stones. On the foundation stones were inscribed the names of the twelve apostles of the Lamb. The apostles were the foundation of the city of God, the new Jerusalem.

Jesus sent his Holy Spirit to the apostles who were guided into all truth (John 16:13). When we obey the teachings of the apostles recorded for us as these holy scriptures, then we will become part of the household of God and citizens in this great and glorious city of God. As the apostle Paul said to the Ephesians,

19 Consequently, you are no longer foreigners and strangers, but fellow citizens with God's people and also members of his household, 20 built on the foundation of the apostles and prophets, with Christ Jesus himself as the chief cornerstone. 21 In him the whole building is joined together and rises to become a holy temple in the Lord. 22 And in him you too are being built together to become a dwelling in which God lives by his Spirit. (Ephesians 2:19-22).

The inclusion of the names of the **twelve sons of Israel** with the **names of the twelve apostles** shows the ultimate fulfillment of God's plan. The faithful people of God from **both covenants** are part of God's family and are in fellowship with the Lord. [23]

9

THE TIME IS NEAR

*³ Blessed is the one who reads aloud the words of this prophecy and blessed are those who hear it and take to heart what is written in it, because **the time is near**. (Revelation 1:3).*

The Great White Throne

So now we see the central feature of this scene, the Great White Throne. It is judgment day when all humanity will give account for their lives on earth.

¹¹ Then I saw a great white throne and him who was seated on it. The earth and the heavens fled from his presence, and there was no place for them. ¹² And I saw the dead, great and small, standing before the throne, and books were opened. Another book was opened, which is the book of life. The dead were judged according to what they had done as recorded in the books. (Revelation 20:11-12).

The Old Heaven and Earth Will Pass Away; All Things will be Made New

²⁵In the beginning you laid the foundations of the earth, and the heavens are the work of your hands.

26 They will perish, but you remain;
  they will all wear out like a garment.
Like clothing you will change them
  and they will be discarded.
27 But you remain the same,
  and your years will never end. (Psalm 102:25-27).

10 But the day of the Lord will come like a thief. The heavens will disappear with a roar; the elements will be destroyed by fire, and the earth and everything done in it will be laid bare.

11 Since everything will be destroyed in this way, what kind of people ought you to be? You ought to live holy and godly lives 12 as you look forward to the day of God and speed its coming. That day will bring about the destruction of the heavens by fire, and the elements will melt in the heat. 13 But in keeping with his promise we are looking forward to a new heaven and a new earth, where righteousness dwells.

13 But in keeping with his promise we (God's people, those redeemed by Christ) *are looking forward to a new heaven and a new earth, where righteousness dwells. 14 So then, dear friends, since you are looking forward to this, make every effort to be found spotless, blameless and at peace with him.24 (2 Peter 3:10-14).*

A New Heaven and a New Earth; The New Jerusalem, the Bride of the Lamb *(God's people, those redeemed by Christ)25*

In the Old Testament, the prophet Isaiah prophesied about the kingdom of God and describes what to expect when the new heavens and new earth appear. It is thought that Isaiah lived mid to late 8th Century BC.

17 "See, I will create new heavens and a new earth. The former things will not be remembered, nor will they come to mind. 18 But be glad and rejoice forever   in what I will create, for I will create Jerusalem to be a delight and its people a joy. *¹⁹ I will rejoice over Jerusalem and take delight in my people; the sound of weeping and of crying will be heard in it no more.* *²⁰ "Never again will there be in it an infant who lives but a few days, or an old man who does not live out his years; the one who dies at a hundred will be thought a mere child; the one who fails to reach a hundred will be considered accursed.* *²¹ They will build houses and dwell in them; they will plant vineyards and eat their fruit.* *²² No longer will they build houses and others live in them, or plant and others eat. For as the days of a tree, so will be the days of my people; my chosen ones will long enjoy the work of their hands.* *²³ They will not labor in vain, nor will they bear children doomed to misfortune; for they will be a people blessed by the LORD, they and their descendants with them.* *²⁴ Before they call I will answer; while they are still speaking I will hear.* *²⁵ The wolf and the lamb will feed together, and the lion will eat straw like the ox, and dust will be the serpent's food. They will neither harm nor destroy on all my holy mountain," says the LORD.* (Isaiah 65:17-25).

"As the new heavens and the new earth that I make will endure before me," declares the LORD, "so will your name and descendants endure." (Isaiah 66:22).

The date of John's Revelation on the Isle of Patmos may have been AD 81-96. With 800-900 years or so between, note the similarities of that vision to the prophet Isaiah's.

The one who is victorious I will make a pillar in the temple of my God. Never again will they leave it. I will write on them the name of my God and the name of the city of my God, **the new Jerusalem, which is coming down out of heaven from my God;** *and I will also write on them my new name.* (Revelation 3:12).

21 ¹Then I saw "a new heaven and a new earth," for the first heaven and the first earth had passed away, and there was no longer any sea. ²I saw *the Holy City, the new Jerusalem, coming down out of heaven from God, prepared as a bride beauty-fully dressed for her husband. ³ And I heard a loud voice from the throne saying, "Look! God's dwelling place is now among the people, and he will dwell with them. They will be his people, and God himself will be with them and be their God. ⁴ 'He will* wipe every tear from their eyes. There will be no more death or mourning or crying or pain, for the old order of things has passed away." ⁵ He who was seated on the throne said, "I am making everything new!" Then he said, "Write this down, for these words are trustworthy and true." ⁶ He said to me: "It is done. I am the Alpha and the Omega, the Beginning and the End. To the thirsty I will give water without cost from the spring of the water of life. ⁷ Those who are victorious will inherit all this, and I will be their God and they will be my children.* (Revelation 21:1-7).

Though John is impressed with the new heaven and the new earth, his attention is immediately directed to that which is central in the vision, "the holy city, new Jerusalem, coming down from God out of heaven, prepared as a bride adorned for her husband.

Because the church, the body of Christ, is considered under the symbolism of a bride in the New Testament in contrast to Israel as the wife of Jehovah, some have attempted to limit the new Jerusalem as having reference only to the church. However, the church on earth is made up of God's people, as the tabernacle in the wilderness was where God was with his people. The point to remember is that the new Jerusalem is made up of God's people from every age, as Abraham *"was looking forward to the city with foundations, whose architect and builder is God."* (Hebrews 11:10).

Among the many marvelous scenes John witnessed was that of Revelation 21, "the holy city, new Jerusalem, coming down from God out of heaven, prepared as a bride adorned for her husband," (21:2). In 21:9, this glorious city is identified as the Bride, the wife of the Lamb. The glorified church, then, is both a *city* and a *bride*. She is "the city of

God" in that she represents the sum of perfected individuals. In her love and unity, she is the "Bride."

God Will Dwell with His People

As John beheld the vision of the new heaven and the new earth and the lovely new Jerusalem, he heard a great voice from heaven giving the spiritual significance of this scene. This is the last of twenty-one times "a great voice" or "a loud voice" is mentioned in the book of Revelation. The fact that the voice is great implies that the subsequent revelation is important and authoritative. The voice declares, *"Look! God's dwelling place is now among the people, and he will dwell with them. They will be his people, and God himself will be with them and be their God."*

The presence of God in scripture frequently implies fellowship and blessing. Here it is stated that the inhabitants of the new Jerusalem will be the people of God and that God will not only be with them but will also be their God, a thought which is often repeated in the scripture.

The emphasis here is on the comfort of God, not on the sadness of the saints. In 21:4, the tears seem to refer to tears shed on earth as the saints endured suffering for Christ's sake, rather than tears shed in heaven because of human failure. This is in keeping with the rest of the passage which goes on to say that other aspects of human sorrow such as death, sadness, crying, or pain will also be no more in existence. The summary given at the end of the verse is, *"The former things are passed away."*

The scriptures make plain that not only the old earth and heaven pass away but also all the sufferings and sorrows associated with it which would stain the beauty in the new heaven and new earth. The church collectively is before us as the *"Bride."* Then the individual's yearning for Christ's appearing is expressed in the second *"Come."*

[17] The Spirit and the bride say, "Come!" And let the one who hears say, "Come!" Let the one who is thirsty come; and let the one who wishes take the free gift of the water of life. (Revelation 22:17).

John's reply to Christ expresses the desire of the bride all down through the ages, *"Come, Lord Jesus."*

10

ANSWERS TO CONTEMPLATE AND SPECULATE

What Do You Think?

WHEN ALL IS SAID AND DONE, THE ONLY THING WE KNOW about heaven is what the Bible says. And we know that God has prepared something for us that we cannot even imagine. So we are left to contemplate and speculate and read what a few experts have to say on the subject. I've read some of the things on the Internet...watched some of the videos on YouTube...seen some of the programs on TV that are only speculative and perhaps create more questions.

Rather than ask the common questions, let's look at some of the answers revealed in prophecy.

The Revelation of Jesus Christ

To reiterate from earlier in our studies: 'Revelation' means to expose in full view what was formerly hidden, veiled, or secret" (Expositor's Bible Commentary). This is a significant beginning to our study. The book of Revelation is revealing something that previously was concealed. Revelation is not code. Revelation is not hidden language. To suggest such violates the very name of the book. This is the book of unveiling. This is the book of revealing, not concealing. This information also sets up our filter for our interpretation method. This book is explaining things that were previously hidden. While we do not know for certain yet, our most likely source would be Old Testament prophecies that were shrouded in mystery that the book is going to make plain. It is noted by all scholars that Revelation borrows heavily from the images of the Old Testament. Therefore, our interpretative model should be that the book of Revelation is an explanation of those Old Testament images. When we read language in Revelation that is found in the Old Testament, we need to go back to the origin of the image and understand it in its proper context. Then we can see how the book of Revelation is shedding light or revealing information about that prophecy. It is not "revelations," but "revelation." One unveiling of the things hidden in the past.

Listen to the prophet, Isaiah, speaking about Jesus and the new heaven and new earth:

A shoot will come up from the stump of Jesse (Jesus);
from his roots a Branch will bear fruit.
² The Spirit of the LORD will rest on him—
the Spirit of wisdom and of understanding,
the Spirit of counsel and of might,
the Spirit of the knowledge and fear of the LORD—
³ and he will delight in the fear of the LORD.

He will not judge by what he sees with his eyes,
or decide by what he hears with his ears;
⁴ but with righteousness he will judge the needy,
with justice he will give decisions for the poor of the earth.
He will strike the earth with the rod of his mouth;
with the breath of his lips he will slay the wicked.
⁵ Righteousness will be his belt
and faithfulness the sash around his waist.

*⁶ **The wolf will live with the lamb,***
the leopard will lie down with the goat,
the calf and the lion and the yearling together;

and a little child will lead them.
⁷ *The cow will feed with the bear,*
　　their young will lie down together,
　　and the lion will eat straw like the ox.
⁸ *The infant will play near the cobra's den,*
　　and the young child will put its hand into the viper's nest.
⁹ *They will neither harm nor destroy*
　　on all my holy mountain,
for the earth will be filled with the knowledge of the Lord
　　as the waters cover the sea.

¹⁰ *In that day the Root of Jesse* (Jesus) *will stand as a banner for the peoples; the nations will rally to him, and his resting place will be glorious.* (Isaiah 11:1-10).

"See, I will create
　　new heavens and a new earth.
The former things will not be remembered,
　　nor will they come to mind.
¹⁸ *But be glad and rejoice forever*
　　in what I will create,
*for **I will create Jerusalem to be a delight***
　　and its people a joy.
¹⁹ *I will rejoice over Jerusalem*
　　and take delight in my people;
the sound of weeping and of crying
　　will be heard in it no more.

²⁰ **"Never again will there be in it**
　　an infant who lives but a few days,
　　or an old man who does not live out his years;
the one who dies at a hundred
　　will be thought a mere child;

93

the one who fails to reach a hundred
will be considered accursed.
²¹ ***They will build houses and dwell in them;***
they will plant vineyards and eat their fruit.
²² No longer will they build houses and others live in them,
or plant and others eat.
For as the days of a tree,
so will be the days of my people;
my chosen ones will long enjoy
the work of their hands.
²³ They will not labor in vain,
nor will they bear children doomed to misfortune;
for they will be a people blessed by the L*ORD*,
they and their descendants with them.
²⁴ Before they call I will answer;
while they are still speaking I will hear.
²⁵ ***The wolf and the lamb will feed together,***
and the lion will eat straw like the ox,
and dust will be the serpent's food.
They will ***neither harm nor destroy***
on all my holy mountain,"
says the L*ORD*. (Isaiah 65:17-25).

Because of Sin

Just think about it -- because of sin, humanity is dying. Since Eden, we are sick, hurting, weak, sad, ashamed, afraid, addicted, hopeless, jealous, envious, selfish, greedy, immoral, hateful, bigoted, cruel beyond belief to animals, children and one another.

Because of sin -- we suffer natural disasters from devastating storms, fires, ice, floods, volcanoes, winds, famines, plagues, pestilence, and the cruelties of war.

Because of sin -- women give birth to their babies in pain and loss of life; and we grieve over little ones who die in the womb. Some may even grieve over killing their little ones in the womb. Or not.

Because of sin -- our present bodies are mortal and susceptible to age-related deterioration, loss of limb and body parts, crooked or broken bones, wrinkled faces, mental disorders, blindness, deafness, deformities, heart problems, suicide, cancer, and other deadly diseases.

Because of sin -- we war against gravity with falls and drownings, ships sinking, and plane crashes; with automobiles killing little children and wrecking property.

There will be NONE of those things in heaven! Hallelujah!

Isaiah prophesied some answers for our contemplation:

1. The New Jerusalem (those redeemed by Christ) will be a delight, and its people a joy to the Lord.
2. The sound of weeping and crying will be no more.
3. We will not remember the sadness on earth.
4. There will be children, but no more dying infants.
5. We will be ageless.
6. We will never worry or be afraid.
7. Jesus will be a glorious banner to all the nations, and we will rally to him.
8. Jesus will hear our words before we finish speaking.
9. We will be filled with knowledge of the Lord.
10. There will be work to do, and we will long enjoy it.
11. There will be animals who live in peace together, and they will not harm children.
12. We will have EVERYTHING we need, and MORE, to keep us happy throughout eternity.

We Shall Marvel at Jesus

¹⁰ on the day he comes **to be glorified in his holy people and to be marveled at among all those who have believed.** *This includes you, because you believed our testimony to you.* (2 Thessalonians 1:10).

I have seen Jesus only in my imagination. He probably had the characteristics of the tribe of Judah, because he was a Jew. He probably wore the common clothing of first century AD with sandals dusty from walking dusty roads from place to place.

That's not all I can see with my mind's eye. I see the image of my savior being whipped, scourged, cursed, and spit upon. I see him carrying his cross to the hill of Golgotha bent, weak and bloody (John 19:12). I see him hanging on that rugged cross almost unconscious with pain and humiliation. Many of those images in my mind have been created by the movie, *"The Passion of the Christ."* Maybe you saw it too. I wept during that movie because those scenes were very hard to watch.

But John, who witnessed the revelation, now he's another story. John was one of Jesus' disciples; one that he loved. He walked many of the same dusty roads and witnessed the healings and the miracles. He was familiar with the expressions of Jesus' face; his gentleness with children, and his disgust with the money changers in the temple. John reclined against Jesus as they supped together, and he allowed Jesus to wash his feet. And, yes, he saw Jesus, the Christ, hanging on that cross. He even took Jesus' mother, Mary, home with him after the cross.

Paul said we will marvel at Jesus. Like John in his dirty old clothes watching that revelation on the Isle of Patmos. And no wonder; listen to John's description of what he saw:

¹ On the Lord's Day I was in the Spirit, and I heard behind me a loud voice like a trumpet, ¹² I turned around to see the voice that was speaking to me. And when I turned I saw seven golden lampstands, ¹³ and among the lampstands was someone like a son of man, dressed in a robe reaching *down to his feet and with a golden sash around his chest. ¹⁴ The hair on his head was white like wool, as white as snow, and his eyes were like blazing fire. ¹⁵ His feet were like bronze glowing in a furnace, and his voice was like the sound of rushing waters. ¹⁶ In his right hand he held seven stars, and coming out of his mouth was a sharp, double-edged sword. His face was like the sun shining in all its brilliance. ¹⁷ When I saw him, I fell at his feet as though dead. Then he placed his right hand on me and said: "Do not be afraid. I am the First and the Last. ¹⁸ I am the Living One; I was dead, and now look, I am alive for ever and ever!* (Revelation 1:10; 12-18).*

Will we marvel at him? Will we fall at his feet as though dead? Perhaps, because he will be more amazing, wonderful, and marvelous than anybody or anything we have ever seen before!
But not only that.

We Shall Be Like Him

If we read some of the scriptures when Jesus spoke about the resurrection, and combine the things he said, we may realize a few more answers. Yes, it is speculation, but consider the words of the scriptures as they are being revealed.

See what great love the Father has lavished on us, that we should be called children of God! And that is what we are! The reason the world does not know us is that it did not know him. ² Dear friends, now we are **children of God**, *and what we will be has not yet been made known. But we know that when Christ appears,* **we shall be like him**, *for we shall see him as he is. ³ All who have this hope in him purify themselves, just as he is pure.* (1 John 3:1, 2).

Jesus said to her (Martha), *"I am the resurrection and the life. The one who believes in me will live, even though they die;* (John 11:25, parentheses mine, SM).

97

*33 Now then, at the resurrection whose wife will she be, since the seven were married to her?" 34 Jesus replied, "The people of this age marry and are given in marriage. 35 But those who are considered worthy of taking part in the age to come and **in the resurrection from the dead will neither marry nor be given in marriage, 36 and they can no longer die; for they are like the angels. They are God's children,** since they are children of the resurrection.* (Luke 20:33-36).

Think about the resurrected body of Jesus before he ascended into heaven. When he appeared to his disciples, they were frightened thinking he was a ghost, but he showed them his body.

30 When he was at the table with them, he took bread, gave thanks, broke it and began to give it to them. 31 Then their eyes were opened and they recognized him, and he disappeared from their sight --

*36 While they were still talking about this, Jesus himself stood among them and said to them, "Peace be with you." 37 They were startled and frightened, thinking they saw a ghost. 38 He said to them, "Why are you troubled, and why do doubts rise in your minds? 39 **Look at my hands and my feet. It is I myself! Touch me and see; a ghost does not have flesh and bones, as you see I have." 40 When he had said this, he showed them his hands and feet. 41 And while they still did not believe it because of joy and amazement, he asked them, "Do you have anything here to eat?" 42 They gave him a piece of broiled fish, 43 and **he took it and ate it in their presence.**

44 He said to them, "This is what I told you while I was still with you. Everything must be fulfilled that is written about me in the Law of Moses, the Prophets and the Psalms."

45 Then he opened their minds so they could understand the Scriptures. (Luke 24:30-31; 36-45).

²⁶ A week later his disciples were in the house again, and Thomas was with them. Though the doors were locked, Jesus came and stood among them and said, "Peace be with you!" ²⁷ Then he said to Thomas, "Put your finger here; see my hands. Reach out your hand and put it into my side. Stop doubting and believe." (John 20:26, 27).

After reading the previous scriptures, please notice some of the things that Jesus said after he was resurrected. He was in a resurrected body that was like that of his body before his death. But this body was glorified as our bodies will be glorified after our resurrection from the dead, or when we are changed from mortal to immortal at his second coming.

In the parable of Luke 16:19-31, the rich man and Lazarus both died. Lazarus was **carried by angels** to the side of Abraham.

Read Hebrews 11, the chapter of faith in action. We can read of these men and women of faith in the Old Testament. In chapter 12, the writer begins with,

*Therefore, since we are **surrounded by such a great cloud of witnesses**, let us throw off everything that hinders and the sin that so easily entangles. And let us run with perseverance the race marked out for us, ² fixing our eyes on Jesus, the pioneer and perfecter of faith. For the joy set before him he endured the cross, scorning its shame, and sat down at the right hand of the throne of God. ³ Consider him who endured such opposition from sinners, so that you will not grow weary and lose heart.* (Hebrews 12:1-3).

1. Jesus said that we will be immortal like angels and will live forever.
2. When we die, angels carry us to heaven.
3. If we know Abraham, and we are surrounded by a "great cloud of witnesses," we may know everyone!
4. John, who saw the visions in Revelation, said that we shall be like the resurrected Jesus.

5. We will be pure as he is pure.
6. He could pass through a door.
7. He could disappear from their sight and reappear.
8. The resurrected Jesus ate food with his disciples.
9. He showed them his wounds from the crucifixion and showed them that he had flesh and bones.
10. He said that in the resurrection, we will be like the angels, neither marrying nor giving in marriage, so we will not be sexual beings.

We Shall See the Face of God!

Jesus said, *"Blessed are the pure in heart,*
   for they will see God." (Matthew 5:8).

In the Old Testament, Moses begged God to see his glory. He was allowed to see God's back one time (Exodus 33:19-23), but God has not shown his face to his people. It has always been considered the pinnacle of righteousness to be able to see God's face. David longed to see the face of God. (Psalm 17:15). All God's people longed to see his face (Psalm 24:6; 105:4); so much so that the desire to see God's face became a priestly blessing:

22 The LORD said to Moses, 23 "Tell Aaron and his sons, 'This is how you are to bless the Israelites. Say to them:

24 The LORD bless you
   and keep you;
25 the LORD make his face shine on you
   and be gracious to you;
26 the LORD turn his face toward you
   and give you peace."' (Numbers 6:22-26).

Returning to John's revelation, *⁴ **They will see his face,** and his name will be on their foreheads. ⁵ There will be no more night. They will not need the light of a lamp or the light of the sun, for the Lord God will give them light. And they will reign for ever and ever.* (Revelation 22:4).

We Shall Again Have Access to the Tree of Life

God has given us the breath of life, our earthly life, the water of life, the path of life, the light of life, the way of life, the bread of life, the word of life, the fountain of life, a covenant of life, the gracious gift of life, an indestructible life, the book of life, the river of life, the tree of life, and in the resurrection, we will be raised to eternal life. What was taken away from mankind because of sin, will be returned to us for eternity.

*Whoever has ears, let them hear what the Spirit says to the churches. To the one who is victorious, I will give the right to eat from the **tree of life**, which is in the paradise of God.* (Revelation 2:7).

*Then the angel showed me the river of the **water of life**, as clear as crystal, flowing from the throne of God and of the Lamb ² down the middle of the great street of the city. On each side of the river stood **the tree of life**, bearing twelve crops of fruit, yielding its fruit every month. And the leaves of the tree are for the healing of the nations.* (Revelation 22:1-5).

We Can't Even Imagine...

⁹ However, as it is written:

"What no eye has seen,
*   what no ear has heard,*
and what no human mind has conceived" —
*   the things God has prepared for those who love him—*

¹⁰ these are the things God has revealed to us by his Spirit.

The Spirit searches all things, even the deep things of God. [11] For who knows a person's thoughts except their own spirit within them? In the same way no one knows the thoughts of God except the Spirit of God.[12] What we have received is not the spirit of the world, but the Spirit who is from God, so that we may understand what God has freely given us. (1 Corinthians 2:9-12).

[20] *Now to him who is able to do immeasurably more than all we ask or imagine, according to his power that is at work within us, [21] to him be glory in the church and in Christ Jesus throughout all generations, for ever and ever! Amen.* (Ephesians 3:20).

I Stand Amazed

Charles H. Gabriel (1905) [26]

I stand amazed in the presence
Of Jesus the Nazarene,
And wonder how He could love me,
A sinner, condemned, unclean.

Refrain:
How marvelous! How wonderful!
And my song shall ever be:
How marvelous! How wonderful!
Is my Savior's love for me!

For me it was in the garden
He prayed: "Not My will, but Thine."
He had no tears for His own griefs,
But sweat drops of blood for mine.

In pity angels beheld Him,
And came from the world of light
To comfort Him in the sorrows
He bore for my soul that night.

He took my sins and my sorrows,
He made them His very own;
He bore the burden to Calv'ry,
And suffered and died alone.

When with the ransomed in glory
His face I at last shall see,
'Twill be my joy through the ages
To sing of His love for me.

11

AFTERWORD

We Have Come Full Circle

WE HAVE COME FULL CIRCLE FROM THE BEGINNING TO the end. This is what we studied:

1. THE CREATION OF GOD - God's creation, the beginning of the heavens and the earth.
2. THE ATTRIBUTES OF GOD - The omni-attributes of God; his omnipotence, omniscience and omni-presence: this all-powerful, all-knowing, and always everywhere three-in-one Father, Son, and Holy Spirit.
3. THE WORD OF GOD - The Bible as God's word as the source of our understanding and hope.
4. THE KINGDOM OF GOD – God's reign on earth and in heaven.
5. THE SON OF GOD - The glory of Jesus Christ coming down from heaven to be a sacrifice for our sins.
6. THE PLAN OF GOD - What the Bible says about Christian eschatology, the study of "end times."
7. THE NEW CREATION OF GOD - John's Revelation of his vision of heaven. We will be reading and learning about the *new heavens and the new earth.* (Revelation 21). You may be familiar with many of these verses, but I urge you to step into

a new vision of things-to-come and investigate with pure eyes everything you have learned in the past and thought you knew about heaven.

8. THE PROMISE OF GOD - Our faith and hope in God's promise that he wants to be with his children.

9. What major religions think about heaven.

10. Unusual near-death experiences.

But not only that.

The Beginning and The End

We saw the beginning of creation (Genesis 1-3), and the ending of God's creation as it is now (2 Peter 3:10-13).

We saw the beginning of the new heavens and new earth. (Revelation 21).

But not only that.

We saw the creation of man and woman and the union of the marriage relationship. (Genesis 2:23-25)

God's relationship with his people has always been as their husband. (Isaiah 54:5-8; Hosea2:19-20).

We saw the relationship of Christ and the church as his wife. (Ephesians 5:21-32).

We saw John's vision that the New Jerusalem (God's redeemed family), is as a bride coming down out of heaven from God, prepared and beautifully dressed for her husband (Revelation 21:2, 9-10).

But not only that.

We saw the serpent, Satan, was in the Garden of Eden to destroy the purity of mankind's relationship with God. (Genesis 3:1-6; 13-16).

We saw that Jesus ruined Satan's plans by his death on the cross to restore mankind to holiness. (Romans 5:17; Romans 8:2; 2 Timothy 1:10; Hebrews 2:9).

We saw John's visions that the dragon, Satan, that serpent of old, and his angels were defeated by our war angel, Michael, and was bound during Christ's reign (Revelation 12:7-9; 20:2).

We saw that devil Satan and his angels were cast into the lake of fire forever. (Revelation 20:9-10).

But not only that.

Although created by God, the Garden of Eden was not perfect, and apparently it was not meant to be. God apparently always had something more in mind for humanity.

Adam's and Eve's sins in the garden separated them from God and banished them from the garden and from the tree of life. But before the creation of the world, God had already made a way to reconcile humanity to himself by the sacrifice of his son, Jesus.

The temporary kingdom of God on earth is the body of people redeemed by God through Jesus Christ.

Physical death is not something to be feared by Christians. The body of people redeemed by God have a mansion waiting that Christ has prepared for us. Those who are faithful to the end will live eternally with God.

Heaven coming down is the scene of John's revelation when God is planning to live with his people in the new heavens and new earth -- a relationship that is like a Father and his children -- like a husband and his wife -- the most intimate of all relationships will be ours when we are in the presence of the triune God.

[13] Then I heard a voice from heaven say, "Write this: Blessed are the dead who die in the Lord from now on." (Revelation 14:13).

APPENDICES

APPENDIX A
EIGHT VERSIONS OF HEAVEN

What Major Religions Think About Heaven [27]

THAT PART OF THE HUMAN BEING THAT SURVIVES DEATH is known in Christianity, Judaism, and Islam as the *soul or spirit,* the very essence of the individual person that must answer for its earthly deeds, good or bad.

However, all the major faiths believe that after the spirit has left the body, it moves on to another existence. Some faiths contend that it ascends to a paradise or descends into a hell. Others believe it may achieve a rebirth into another physical body or may merge with the Divine in an eternal unity.

With all their diversity of beliefs, the major religions are in accord in one great teaching: Human beings are immortal, and their spirit comes from a divine world and may eventually return there. Since the earliest forms of spiritual expression, this is the great promise and hope that religions have offered to their followers. It is the believer's eternal answer to the cynicism of the materialist who shouts that there is no afterlife, that death is the end.

Traditional Christianity, Judaism, and Islam envision a resurrection of a spiritual body at a time of final judgment, but generally speaking, the soul is of greater value and purpose than the physical body it inhabited while on Earth. The material shell within which humans dwell during their lifetime is nothing other than clay or ashes into which God has breathed the breath of life. The physical body is a temporary possession that a human has, not what a person is.

Most of the major world religions hold the belief that how a person has conducted himself or herself while living on Earth will greatly influence his or her soul's ultimate destiny after physical death. In fact, many teachings state that the only reason for birth into the material world is the opportunity to prepare for the soul's destiny in the immaterial worlds. And what is more, how one meets the challenges of life on Earth, whether one chooses to walk a path of good or evil, or not, determines how that soul will be treated after death. All the seeds that one has sown throughout his or her lifetime, good or bad, will be harvested in the afterlife.

Regardless of one's religious background, it is in the presence of death that all humans find themselves face to face with the single greatest mystery of their existence: Does life extend beyond the grave? Whether one believes in a supernatural heavenly kingdom, the inescapable laws of karma, or a state of eternal bliss, death remains a dreadful force beyond one's control. For untold millions of men and women the ceremonies of religion provide their only assurance that life goes on when the darkness of physical death envelops them.

The core of the Christian faith is the belief in the resurrection of Jesus after his death on the cross and the promise of life everlasting to all who accept his divinity and believe in him. Because Christianity rose out of Judaism, the teachings of Jesus as recorded in the gospels reflect many of the Jewish beliefs of the soul and the afterlife, primarily that a reunion of body and soul will be accomplished in the next world.

The accounts of the appearance of Jesus to his apostles after his resurrection show how completely they believed that they beheld him in the flesh, even to the extreme of the skeptical Thomas placing his fingertips into the still-open wounds of the crucifixion. *"A spirit does not have flesh and bones as you see that I have,"* Jesus told them. Then, to prove his physicality still further, he asks if they have anything for him to eat.

Paul the apostle, and once avid persecutor of Christians, received his revelation from the voice of Jesus within a blinding light while he was traveling on the road to Damascus. He discovered it to be a challenge to convince others in the belief in the physical resurrection of the dead when he preached in Athens. Although the assembled Athenians listened politely to his message of a new faith, they mocked him and walked away when he began to speak of dead bodies standing up and being reborn.

Judaism

As one of the oldest and most influential religions in existence, Judaism might be expected to be the source of our most profound notions of heaven, but it isn't. In fact, the Torah doesn't mention the afterlife at all, leaving much of what happens to personal interpretation. For the Jewish people, the greatest emphasis is on life itself, and respecting that life. Two typical positions are those of the Pharisees, who believed that there was an implied notion of an afterlife, and the Sadducees, who pointed out that there was no evidence of such.

Over the millennia, Jews have come to believe in various versions of heaven, some of which occur after the Messiah comes and involve the righteous dead coming back to life. Judaism differs from many other monotheistic religions in that there is no set concept of the afterlife.

While some Jews believe in a heaven of sorts, most don't believe in hell, at least not in the Christian sense of it. However, resurrection of the dead upon the arrival of the Messiah is a pretty common belief, as long as you have been good during your life. Those who were not so good prior to their death will not be resurrected to enjoy the world to come, which is supposed to be perfect.

Christianity

It is a core belief for Christians that how you live your life will affect the quality your death. Basically, those who were good people and lived by God's rules will ascend to heaven, presumably where everything will be perfect. Those who were bad, on the other hand, will be tossed into the fiery pits of hell, where they will be forced to suffer for all eternity.

Catholics, however, have an escape: they also believe in purgatory, in addition to heaven and hell. Purgatory is a place of temporary punishment for those who have yet to confess their sins.

According to the Catechism of the Catholic Church: All who die in God's grace and friendship, but still imperfectly purified, are indeed assured of their eternal salvation; but after death they undergo purification, so as to achieve the holiness necessary to enter the joy of heaven. People in purgatory are already with God, yet they need our prayers to help them to be purified of all the effects of sin and ready to see God face-to-face.

Generally speaking, the Christian understanding of heaven is one of singing and rejoicing before God in the "new heavens and a new earth." It also reflects Christianity's roots in Judaism because this new heaven contains a city called New Jerusalem. There are elaborate descriptions of the city in the Bible's Revelation. New Jerusalem has a wall and twelve gates, and on each gate is the name of one of the tribes of Israel along with an angel. There are also twelve foundations, one each for the twelve apostles.

The structure itself is made of many different precious stones, some of which have not yet been identified on this earth. There is a river of "the water of life," which flows from God's throne, and trees of life line the banks of the river and produce fruit every month.

Believers will have God's name written on their foreheads, and all pain, tears, and death will disappear forever.

Islam

Similarly to Judaism, Islam believes that on the Last Day (also known as Day of Judgment), Allah will resurrect everyone who has died. At that point, they will be judged and sent to either Paradise or Hell. Those who died believing that "There is no true god but God, and Muhammad is the messenger (prophet) of God," will be held in very high graces, and will be guaranteed a beautiful eternity.

But where the Jews will have a relatively uneventful waiting period before their possible resurrection, Muslims don't have it so easy, especially if they've been bad during life. It is believed that these people will literally suffer every single second of every single day until judgment day, while those who behaved appropriately while alive will be in ultimate peace until it's time for them to head to Paradise.

Unlike the Christian's idea of heaven, Islam's Paradise is fairly decadent. It consists of lofty mansions, delicious food and drink. The Islamic version of heaven is a paradise for those whose good works have outweighed the bad as determined by the straight path laid out in the Quran.

Hinduism

Eastern religions don't really have notions of heaven like those in the West. Instead, they usually offer some kind of release from illusion and suffering in the present world.

Hinduism is a religion that believes in reincarnation based on karma. In Hinduism, there are three types of karma: that of past lives, that of the present life, and that of the lives not yet lived. This karma will determine in what entity they will be born in their next life, with the goal of eventually being released from the rebirth cycle to reach moksha.

Moksha is a state of enlightenment that can only be achieved through a series of good deeds from one life to the next. Once Moksha is reached, there is no more suffering and ultimate self-realization comes into focus during that life. From there, with the rebirth cycle broken, the final step is Ioka (heaven).

The Hindu Upanishads are philosophical portions of the Vedas, Hinduism's oldest sacred text, and in them the notions of the self and afterlife are developed. According to the Upanishads, our actions connect us to this world of appearances, which is in fact illusory. What is real is Brahman, the ultimate reality that transcends our sensory experiences. Unfortunately, we live in ignorance of Brahman and act according to our illusions. This action, karma, causes us to participate in the cycle of death and rebirth, samsara, from which it's difficult to escape. So, if you can escape your ignorance and realize that ultimately you are not you but Brahman itself, then you can achieve release from the cycle of death and rebirth.

Buddhism

One of the four noble truths of the Buddha is that suffering is caused by desire, the desire to have but also the desire to be. Desire is tanha, or a burning that keeps us caught in the web of illusion that is our ego. The Buddha taught that desire is a flame that burns us, causes suffering, and keeps us tied to the cycle of death and rebirth because the flame continues burning into the next life. What we hope for is Nirvana, or the extinguishing of that flame, which is also the end of suffering.

The Buddhist religion also doesn't see death as an ending, but rather a beginning to a new life through reincarnation. What one will be in their next life is the result of how they lived in their past lives.

A person can be reincarnated in one of the six "realms," as they call them: heaven, hell, human, animal, hungry ghost (the constant state of dissatisfaction), or Asura (the realm of constant fighting).

This being Buddhism, none of the realms are permanent. To Buddhists, there is no death, just a series of lives based on accumulated karma, from one life to the next.

Scientology

A religion created by science fiction writer, L. Ron Hubbard, Scientologists call the soul a "thetan." To them, each thetan is reincarnated over and over again, bouncing from one life to the next, and is billions of years old. When a Scientologist dies, there are no requirements to love and serve others like there is with Christian-based religions, nor is there a judgment period. You just die and wait to pop up in another life. Luckily for Scientologists, they don't believe in heaven or hell, so what they do in this life isn't going to condemn them in the afterlife.

Mormon

Similarly to Christians, Mormons believe in heaven and hell. Where they differ is that Mormons also believe that before the dead can get to heaven, they need to go through some preparation that involves instructions in the spirit world. After awhile, if all is good, their bodies and soul will be together again in heaven for all eternity.

Jehovah's Witnesses

Most of their beliefs are based upon their interpretation of the Bible. Jehovah's Witnesses believe that only 144,000 people will go to heaven and that other people who obey God will live forever on a paradise Earth.

The Bible Says --

Much of what the Bible reveals about heaven are symbolic descriptions that represent or correspond to something to which we can relate. As we consider the above religious beliefs, it is imperative that we compare them to what the Bible says about heaven. No matter how lovely a belief, if it contradicts scripture, it must be released to accept what the Bible reveals.

Acknowledge and take to heart this day that the Lord is God in heaven above and on the earth below. There is no other. (Deuteronomy 4:39).

²² But you have come to Mount Zion, to the city of the living God, the heavenly Jerusalem. You have come to thousands upon thousands of angels in joyful assembly, ²³ to the church of the firstborn, whose names are written in heaven. You have come to God, the Judge of all, to the spirits of the righteous made perfect, ²⁴ to Jesus the mediator of a new covenant, (Hebrews 12:22-24a).

As for reincarnation -- *Just as people are destined to die once, and after that to face judgment,* (Hebrews 9:27).

APPENDIX B
NEAR DEATH EXPERIENCES

Really?

YOU MAY BE WONDERING WHY I WOULD CHOOSE TO address this subject in my writing. I don't blame you. Here you will read why this phenomenon in society became of interest to me.

As a summary before going further, I have come to the uninteresting conclusion that anything that happens in our lives that we cannot explain, but does no harm, and may have beneficial, long-lasting, positive effects on our faith journey should not be ridiculed or challenged but should be held with respect for the ones who live through the experiences.

Until my mother was in her last hours on this earth, I had not given much credit to the many stories of near-death experiences that have been popularized in songs, movies and books. Truly, I still don't know what to think of those accounts because when one talks about dying, going to heaven, and then returning to the realm of the living, it feels a little spooky or unreal.

Yes, you can call me a skeptic in that I often question the answers to those things about which one is only able to speculate. In this case, because there are many unknowns, medically, psychologically, physically, emotionally, and spiritually, we often grasp for something that makes us feel good momentarily.

At ninety-seven years of age, my mom had outlived her parents, brother, extended family, and friends. She had basically lived for me and my children. She was baptized when she was nine years old, and lived a faithful, consecrated life in the Lord. She was indescribably kind and loving, and when goodness was discussed, it had been said, "well, if Virginia doesn't go to heaven, no one will."

She lived with me the last ten years of her life, not because she was suffering from old-age dementia or disabled, but because she was legally blind from macular degeneration. She could only see shadows and needed someone to walk with her at all times.

But she knew nothing about near-death experiences (NDE's). If she had known, she may have been skeptical too. But as her transition into eternity was imminent, with my children and I beside her, she looked into space as if she was watching something unfold before her eyes. She smiled and said, "I see all my friends! I see all my friends!"

Who am I to skeptically deny or question that she saw that beautiful vision? I believe she saw and recognized her friends, and it made her happy in those last hours.

Recorded NDE's For Your Information

Crystal McVea was a self-proclaimed church going skeptic who had a near death experience after complications from pancreatitis. During her time on the emergency room slab, this mother of four from Oklahoma ascended to heaven and discovered there were no emotional tethers in the Kingdom of God. And even though she was new to after-life she was still able to meet the one in charge. McVea told *The Blaze*, "I was very aware that I was in front of the presence of the one true God. I'm a Christian. I believe it was the presence of the Father, and the Son and the Holy Spirit." He then gave her the choice to stay in heaven or return to Earth to her four children and lucrative book deal. [28]

Heaven is for Real is probably the most famous account of a visit to heaven, and it comes to us from **Colton Burpo**, who was only three years old when he died on the operating table during a surgery, went to heaven, and then returned with the knowledge of an unborn sister, Jesus' love of riding a rainbow colored horse across the cloud city of heaven. In

2015, Burpo reiterated his claims to *Charisma News*: "I know there has been a lot of talk about the truth of other heaven stories in the past few days. I just wanted to take a second and let everyone know that I stand by my story found in my book *Heaven is for Real*. I still remember my experience in Heaven."[29]

Annabel Beam suffered a terrible accident at the age of nine when she found herself stuck inside of a hollowed-out cottonwood tree. Luckily she was pulled to safety by firefighters, and a day after the incident Beam told her mother she "sat on Jesus's lap" and talked about how she would be okay. Initially, her mother didn't believe her, but when the nine-year-old dropped some knowledge about her mom's two miscarriages she knew that her daughter had truly been to heaven and wasn't simply suffering from a tree delusion. Beam was miraculously cured of her medical ailments and has since had a movie made about her life, starring Jennifer Garner, called *Miracles From Heaven*.[30]

After drowning on a kayaking trip in 1999, **Mary Neal,** an orthopedic surgeon, swam up to heaven where she spent a good thirty minutes before being resuscitated. Neal believes Jesus held her as she drowned, and that made her feel "more alive" than she had ever felt. Then she felt her consciousness break away from herself and she was "immediately greeted by a group of beings, spirits, people," and after gaining her non-bodily bearings she found herself at "the big arched entryway," and inside she saw "many other spirits, angels, people -- all running around. They were all very busy -- busy doing God's work."[31]

In 2008, **Dr. Eben Alexander** contracted bacterial meningitis of the brain and spent a week in a coma where he took a trip through the afterlife. Rather than be led to heaven by a mysterious being or cluster of light, he entered the afterlife by what he calls the "earthworm's eye view" before the "blinders came off and [revealed] this crisp, ultra-real gateway with beautiful butterflies and flowers, with souls dancing and angels above [him]. There were colors beyond the rainbow and butterflies appeared repeatedly."[32]

Most people who take a trip to the great beyond come back with vague notions that everything felt good, or that there were bright lights and some nice architecture. But not **Oden Hetrick**. Upon returning from his first trip to heaven he wrote a 21-chapter book detailing every inch of heaven. His book fills his readers in on what kind of clothes people wear in heaven: "There are three different garments here: the garment of humility; the robe of righteousness; and the garment of praise. To be fully dressed, we put them on in that order." He also details the appearance of God himself, describing him as some sort of giant. "When God sits on His Throne before a gathering of saints, He makes Himself big enough so that all may easily see Him." [33]

After being T-boned by a teen who ran a red light, **Julie Papievis** found herself in a coma due to a serious stem injury, and she wasn't expected to survive. While doctors and her family debated about how to proceed Papievis became acquainted with heaven. She told the *700 Club*: "It was so vast, and there was no real beginning or end to it. It was just perfect peace. It was like I was home, and I wanted to stay there." But her grandmother wouldn't let Papievis stay in heaven. "My grandmother said, 'No, you can't come with us. You have to go back. Go back and be happy.'" Ten years later, Papievis recovered enough to complete an indoor triathlon. [34]

Don Piper, who was pronounced clinically dead after a car crash in 1989, said he traveled to heaven. After dying in a four-car pileup, Piper found himself "standing at some magnificent gates surrounded by people [he] had known and loved in life." Piper knew he was in heaven. But enough about these gates, does heaven have awesome architecture? He told Bill O'Reilly, "There really are a lot of magnificent structures inside the gate. And at the pinnacle of a great hill beyond them is a bright light." [35]

Possible Explanations for Experiences

Near-death experiences are one of the most puzzling phenomena in psychology. A near-death experience is when a person appears to be clinically 'dead' for a short period – when their heart stops beating, their brain registers no sign of activity, and the other 'vital signs' indicate death – and yet they report a continuation of consciousness. This may happen following a cardiac arrest, for example. For a few seconds or minutes, a person may show no biological signs of life, and yet when they are resuscitated, report a series of remarkable experiences.

NDEs have never been satisfactorily explained in neurobiological terms. Various theories have been suggested, such as hallucinations caused by a lack of oxygen to the brain, undetected brain activity (during the period when the brain appears not to be functioning), the release of endorphins, a psychological 'depersonalization' in response to intense stress, and so on. All these theories have been found to be problematic. For example, oxygen deficiency usually results in chaotic hallucinatory experiences and is associated with confusion and memory loss. NDEs are completely unlike this. They are serene, structured, and well-integrated experiences. In theory, in NDEs people could have a very low level of brain activity which is not picked up by EEG machines. On the other hand, it seems very unlikely that such a low level of brain activity could produce such vivid and intense conscious experiences. If there was any conscious experience, it would surely be dim, vague and confused. In contrast, in NDEs, people often report becoming more alert than normal, with a very clear and intense form of awareness.

Another theory that has been proposed is that NDEs are related to psychedelic chemicals which are naturally produced by the human brain. (Dimethyltryptamine (DMT) is an intense naturally-occurring psychedelic that's also found endogenously in the human body.)

Aiming to study the apparent similarities between the psychedelic substance and NDEs, the researchers gave both DMT and a placebo to 13 participants, then asked them to complete a scale of the characteristics of NDEs.

The results were reported as showing a significant overlap between the two types of experience. As the researchers concluded, "Results revealed significant increases in phenomenological features associated with the NDE, following DMT administration compared to placebo."

This appears to be true, but on closer inspection, the findings of the paper still fall far short of establishing any strong connection between DMT and NDEs.

Of the 16 items in the NDE scale used in the study, 9 items showed a high degree of 'crossover.' These included an 'unearthly environment,' a sense of peace, heightened senses, harmony/unity, altered time perception, feeling of joy, bright light, and standard spiritual experiences.

For example, three of the most salient specific characteristics of NDEs are a feeling of reaching a 'border/point of no return,' 'encountering deceased/religious spirits,' and a life review. In this study, these were among the least reported in DMT experiences.

NDEs are powerfully transformative experiences. After them, a person's values and attitude to life may be completely transformed. People often become less materialistic and more altruistic, less self-oriented and more compassionate. They often feel a new sense of purpose, and their relationships become more authentic and intimate. They report becoming more sensitive to beauty, and more appreciative of everyday things. They also typically report a loss of the fear of death. [36]

Near Death Experience Research Foundation

This is not an endorsement for or against the study of NDE's. But as a matter of interest, NDERF is the largest NDE website in the world with over 4,500 experiences in over 23 languages. Their website is a free public service. They welcome and encourage all people of all backgrounds, nationalities, countries, and religions to read and participate on the website. Their mission is to research and study consciousness experiences and to spread the message of love, unity, and peace around the world. [37]

ABOUT THE AUTHOR

SANDRA MACKEY HAS BEEN A CHRISTIAN FOR OVER 65 years. She lives in Roswell, Georgia, where she retired from a Fortune 200 Corporation in 2016.

Sandra's love of teaching and Bible study has enabled her to dedicate her talents to speaking and writing, and her computer skills have promoted her interest in art, poetry, freelance writing, editing and website design. As an Able Toastmaster, she has been the key-note speaker for inspirational and motivational workshops in eight Southern states.

Her personal website, https://sandramackey.com, is a good landing page for Bible study and additional inspirational resources on her monthly blog, *Webstable Soup*.

Sandra's four children, three grandchildren, one great-granddaughter, and their families are her treasures! She is a member of the North Atlanta Church of Christ.

Other books by Sandra Mackey:
Better Than Gold and Silver
Poems of Love and Faith
The Spirit of Truth
When Righteousness and Peace Kiss

Other Writing Experience:
Contributor - *Chapter Thirteen, An Investigation of Angels,* by Wynelle F. Main
Editor - *Workbook for Spouses of Sex Addicts: Hope for the Journey,* by Françoise Mastroianni, LCPC, SEP, CADC, CCSAS, and Richard Blankenship, LPC, NCC, CCH, CCSAS
Five (5) *L.I.F.E. International Recovery Study Guides*:
- o *General*
- o *For Men*
- o *For Women*
- o *For Spouses*
- o *Facilitators Guide for Men and Women*

Editor - *Lift-Reach-Connect*, a three-year series of magazines for North Atlanta Church of Christ
Consultant - *Return to Innocence*, by Dr. Mark Richardson
Consultant - *52 Days on the Wall*, by Dr. Mark Richardson
Editor - *The Sustainability Edge*, by Suhas Apte and Jagdish N. Sheth
Editor - *A Cry for Relief,* by David A. Wheeler

Social Media:
sandramackey11@gmail.com
https://sandramackey.com
https://www.facebook.com/sandra.mackey1

RECOMMENDED READING

1. *When Christ Comes: The Beginning of the Very Best,* Max Lucado, Copyright © 1999, published by Thomas Nelson, Inc.
2. *Beyond Heaven's Door*, Max Lucado, Copyright © 2013, published by Thomas Nelson, Inc.
3. *The Dawn of the New Creation*, Copyright © 2018 by Brayden Brookshier. www.sermontobook.com.

For a more in-depth study of this subject, check these two websites:
https://www.biblestudytools.com/commentaries/
http://thebookofrevelationmadeclear.com/

ENDNOTES

1 https://www.merriam-webster.com/dictionary.

2 The Holy Bible, New International Version®, NIV®
   Copyright © 1973, 1978, 1984, 2011 by Biblica, Inc.® Used
   by permission. All rights reserved worldwide.

3 ©2016 Billy Graham Evangelistic Association. Used by
   permission. All rights reserved.

4 Excerpt from: https://blog.oxforddictionaries.
   com/2014/12/09/psy-youtube-quintillion/.

5 https://www.math.toronto.edu/mathnet/questionCorner/
   largestnumber.html.

6 https://www.wonderslist.com/10-most-intelligent-people.

7 Excerpt from: https://www.blueletterbible.org/Comm/
   spurgeon_charles/sermons/2201.cfm?a=1103016

8 Excerpts from a previously published work by Sandra
   Mackey, Better Than Gold and Silver, Copyright © 1975,
   Quality Publications.

9 Ibid.

10 The Church in the Power of the Spirit, by Jürgen Moltmann,
   English translation © 1977, SCM Press Ltd.

11 http://preachingsource.com/blog/testifying-to-gospel-
   preaching-jesus-and-the-gospel-in-the-old-testament/.

12 Excerpts from The International Standard Bible Encyclopaedia, Volume III, Hendrickson Publishers, Inc. Edition, 1994.

13 Excerpts from Compton's Interactive Bible NIV. Copyright © 1994, 1995, 1996 SoftKey Multimedia Inc. All Rights Reserved.

14 Ibid.

15 Excerpts from a previously published work by Sandra Mackey, The Spirit of Truth, Copyright © 2011, by Crossbooks.

16 https://www.gotquestions.org/in-but-not-of-world.html.

17 Excerpts from a previously published work by Sandra Mackey, Better Than Gold and Silver, Copyright © 1975, Quality Publications.

18 1 Corinthians 15:24-18

19 https://www.gotquestions.org/in-but-not-of-world.html.

20 Quote by N. T. Wright. https://www.azquotes.com/quote/710908.

21 Spurgeon, "The Heaven of Heavens," 433.

22 Expositor's Bible Commentary.

23 Excerpts from http://thebookofrevelationmadeclear.com/revelation-bible-study/unveiling-the-future.html - Brent Kercheville, Minister for the West Palm Beach, Florida Church of Christ. Used by permission.

24 Excerpts from a previously published work by Sandra Mackey, Better Than Gold and Silver, Copyright © 1975, Quality Publications.

25 (God's people, those redeemed by Christ) parentheses mine. SM

26 I Stand Amazed, Copyright status Public Domain.

27 https://www.encyclopedia.com/science/encyclopedias-almanacs-transcripts-and-maps/how-major-religions-view-afterlife.

28 https://www.simonandschuster.com/books/Waking-Up-in-Heaven/Crystal-McVea/9781476711874.

29 https://en.wikipedia.org/wiki/Heaven_Is_for_Real.

30 http://www.historyvshollywood.com/reelfaces/miracles-from-heaven/.

31 https://www.christianitytoday.com/ct/2012/december-web-only/mary-neal-describes-her-visit-to-gates-of-heaven.html.

32 https://www.newsweek.com/proof-heaven-doctors-experience-afterlife-65327.

33 https://www.odenhetrick.com/read.html.

34 https://www.gobackandbehappy.com/.

35 http://www1.cbn.com/700club/don-piper-90-minutes-heaven.

36 Excerpts from https://www.psychologytoday.com/us/blog/out-the-darkness/201810/near-death-experiences-and-dmt. Used by permission. Copyright Sussex Publishers, LLC. Except as otherwise expressly permitted under copyright law, no copying, redistribution, retransmission, publication or commercial exploitation of downloaded material will be permitted without the express written permission of Sussex Publishers, LLC.

37 https://www.nderf.org/Archives/NDERF_NDEs.html.

CPSIA information can be obtained
at www.ICGtesting.com
Printed in the USA
FSHW011406100619
58908FS